Serbia and Montenegro

Serbia and Montenegro

MICHAEL A. SCHUMAN

Facts On File, Inc.

Nations in Transition: Serbia and Montenegro

Copyright © 2004 by Michael A. Schuman

Facts On File, Inc.
132 West 31st Street
New York NY 10001

Library of Congress Cataloging-in-Publication Data

Schuman, Michael.
　　Serbia and Montenegro / Michael Schuman.
　　　　p. cm.— (Nations in transition)
　　Includes bibliographical references and index.
　　ISBN 0-8160-5054-6 (alk. paper)
　　　　1. Serbia and Montenegro. I. Title. II. Series.
　　DR1940.S38 2004
　　949.7103—dc222003049413

Facts On File books are available at special discounts when purchased in bulk quantities for businesses, associations, institutions, or sales promotions. Please call our Special Sales Department in New York at (212) 967-8800 or (800) 322-8755.

You can find Facts On File on the World Wide Web at
http://www.factsonfile.com

Text design by Erika K. Arroyo
Cover design by Nora Wertz
Maps by Patricia Meschino © Facts On File, Inc.

Printed in the United States of America

MP FOF 10 9 8 7 6 5 4 3 2 1

This book is printed on acid-free paper.

CONTENTS

INTRODUCTION

The country known today as Serbia and Montenegro can be perceived as two nations loosely joined together to make one entity. Serbia and Montenegro were once separate republics of a substantially larger nation, Yugoslavia, which consisted of six republics and existed in one form or another from 1918–92. Of the six republics—Slovenia, Bosnia and Herzegovina, Croatia, Macedonia, Serbia, and Montenegro—Serbia and Montenegro were the closest allies. After the other four Yugoslav republics declared their independence in 1992, Serbia and Montenegro existed as residual Yugoslavia. It was not until 2002 that what remained of Yugoslavia changed its name and became the nation of Serbia and Montenegro.

While the two republics share a common ancestry, there are many differences between them, a major one being size. Serbia has roughly 10 million residents. The much smaller Montenegro has a population of about 650,000. Serbia, consisting of about 54,800 square miles, is about the size of the state of Iowa. Montenegro, with about 8,600 square miles, is similar in size to Massachusetts. Serbia has always been a much more urbane republic than Montenegro, whose residents are rural-based and perceived by most residents of the Balkans as provincial. Serbia's economy, while not the strongest of the former Yugoslav republics, was always much healthier than that of Montenegro, long considered the poorest of the bigger nation's six republics.

In addition, the republic of Serbia includes two autonomous regions, or provinces. One, in the northernmost part of the republic, is Vojvodina. It borders Romania, Croatia, and Hungary. Vojvodina is about 13,300 square miles in size and has about 2 million inhabitants, about 20 percent

of Serbia's total population. While about half the population of Vojvodina consists of ethnic Serbs, a sizable minority—about 340,000 people—
are of Hungarian descent and identify much more with Hungary than
with Serbia.

The other autonomous province is officially called Kosovo and Meto-
hija, but is more familiarly known as Kosovo, and will be referred to as
such in this book. The political situation in Kosovo has been the source
of heated disputes and savage violence with Serbia proper for years.
Located in the extreme southwest of Serbia, along the borders of Albania
and Macedonia, Kosovo is only 6,740 square miles, about the size of met-
ropolitan Los Angeles. However, like Vojvodina, Kosovo is home to
roughly 2 million people, making it the most densely populated region of
Serbia and Montenegro.

About 1.6 million, or roughly 80 percent of Kosovo's population, are
ethnic Albanians who believe in Sunni Islam, as opposed to the Serbs
and Montenegrins, who are Orthodox Christian. Only about 194,000
Kosovans are ethnic Serbs. For that reason some think that Kosovo
should belong to Albania. However, Serbs have strong emotional ties to
Kosovo, as explained further in the history and religion chapters. Some
might even say that Kosovo is the emotional, if not the geographic, heart
of Serbia. It is no surprise that Kosovo has been a source of conflict
among Christian Serbs and Muslim ethnic Albanians.

The people of Serbia and Montenegro—or at least those of Serbia—
have had an image problem since the early 1990s. After four of the
Yugoslav republics declared their independence in 1992, Serbia, under
the leadership of Slobodan Milošević, allegedly aided a campaign of ethnic cleansing by Serbs in the two neighboring republics, Croatia and
Bosnia and Herzegovina. Ethnic cleansing in this case involved clearing
out non-Serbs in areas with a large ethnic Serb population. The Serbs'
manner of conducting this campaign involved military action, concentration camps, and alleged genocide, causing many observers to compare
Serbia in the 1990s to Nazi Germany during World War II. While other
parties involved in the civil war have also been accused of ethnic cleansing, Milošević is thought to have been at the forefront of some of the
most severe incidents.

Then in 1998 Serbia, again under Milošević, attempted to wipe out
the Kosovo Liberation Army, a group of armed Kosovan Albanians who

were seeking independence for Kosovo. Many observers felt the military campaign, in which hundreds were killed and hundreds of thousands lost their homes, was inhumane. Although Serbia and Montenegro are today governed by a respected democracy, Serbs have had a hard time shaking their reputation of brutality from the 1990s. There is an irony in this, since in World War I and especially in World War II, Serbs were the victims of the same types of cruelty their government is said to have been guilty of in the 1990s. Until the breakup of Yugoslavia and the ensuing civil war, Serbs had been viewed by the world's citizens as unfortunate victims of and heroes in the resistance against Nazi Germany.

The Serbo-Croatian Language

One thing Serbia and Montenegro do have in common is language. To the citizens of the rest of the world, the language spoken here is called Serbo-Croatian, which was the name of the official language of Yugoslavia. Since the breakup of Yugoslavia, there is technically no such language. In the name of ethnic pride, residents of Serbia now refer to the language as *Serbian*, while citizens of Croatia call it *Croatian*. In

---

SPEAKING SERBO-CROATIAN

A few Cyrillic characters are written and pronounced as they are in the Latin alphabet, including *a, m,* and *k.* There are several exceptions, however. The letter *j* is pronounced like the consonant *y,* as in *young.* The letters *lj* together sound like the "lli" in *million.* The letters *nj* together take the sound of "ny," as in *canyon,* and the letter *š* is pronounced like "sh," as in *shoe.*

The most complex Latin character of Serbo-Croatian is the letter *c.* In Cyrillic, the character *c* takes the sound of the Latin character *s,* as in *snow.* In the Latin transliteration of Serbo-Croatian, the character *c* can take on three sounds depending how it is written. A *c* with no diacritical mark above it sounds like "ts," as in *bats.* A "ć" takes on the "ch" sound as in *itch.* A single "č" sounds like "ch," as in *church.*

multi-ethnic Bosnia and Herzegovina, the same Serbo-Croatian language is referred to by three different names: Bosnian Serbs call it *Serbian*, Bosnian Croats call it as *Croatian*, and Bosnian Muslims, known as Bosniaks, call it *Bosnian*.

To confuse matters even more, the former Yugoslavs do not write the language with the same alphabet. Croats use the Latin alphabet, with the same 26 letters used in English and four additional letters. Ethnic Albanians in Kosovo and ethnic Hungarians in Vojvodina also write in the Latin alphabet. Serbs, however, write in a 30-letter Cyrillic alphabet, while Montenegrins write using both the Cyrillic and Latin alphabets.

Interestingly, if you should browse through a book or magazine published from 1945 to 1980, it will likely be written in the Latin alphabet. Yugoslavia's leader at that time was Josip Broz, Marshal Tito, who thought it would be beneficial for his compatriots to use a single alphabet. His logic was that it would help unify the different people of a country with so many different nationalities. Sarajevo's leading newspaper, *Oslobođenje* (famous for its uninterrupted publication during the civil war), however, was printed in one language but with both alphabets. Street signs were also often stamped in both alphabets.

As with English family names, Serbo-Croatian surnames utilize suffixes and prefixes to denote various meanings. The most common Serbo-Croatian family names end in *ić*, pronounced like *itch* and translated as "child of." This is analogous to the English *-son*. Women's first names almost always end in either *a* or *ica*, which is pronounced "eet-sa."

In addition, many ethnic minorities shun the Serbo-Croatian language. It is common for many Albanians to speak Albanian and ethnic Hungarians to write and converse in Hungarian.

The Lay of the Land

Because of its location, the southeastern corner of the European continent, Serbia and Montenegro is referred to as the "crossroads of Europe." With main trade routes forged, then railroad lines and highways built through natural river valleys, the nation, especially the Serbian republic, has long been the site of the shortest routes between Europe and the Middle East, Asia, and Africa.

There are numerous important rivers flowing through Serbia and Montenegro. The most famous is the Danube, the second longest river in Europe (the Volga River in Russia is the longest), and immortalized in Johann Strauss's "The Blue Danube" waltz. Its source is in southwestern Germany, and it flows 1,770 miles southeast, with 365 of those miles through Serbia. The Danube forms part of the border between Serbia and Romania before it empties into the Black Sea. It has always had a major connection to Serbia's economic well-being and today serves one of the largest hydroelectric power plants in Europe.

The two other important rivers in Serbia are the Sava and the Morava. The Sava rises in the Julian Alps of Slovenia and flows about 580 miles until it empties into the Danube in the nation's capital city, Belgrade. The Morava forms in the hills of central Serbia and flows for 130 miles, emptying into the Danube east of Belgrade. The most important waterway in Montenegro is the Zeta River, which divides Montenegro into two geographic regions. To the west of the Zeta are mostly barren plains; to the east, in what is known as the Brda, are hills, forests, and pastures. With its 90-mile-long coastline, Montenegro is the only part of the nation bordering the Adriatic Sea.

If you are looking for a land with geographic diversity, Serbia is one place to visit. Most of northern Serbia, including Vojvodina, sits in a region called the Pannonian Plain and, with the exception of some low hills, is flat. South and central Serbia are covered with the North Albanian Alps and Šar Mountains; the Dinaric Alps gird the nation in the west, and the Balkan and Carpathian Mountains ring the country in the east. Many peaks reach more than 6,000 feet in height.

In addition to topography, Serbia has a wide range in its climate. The Pannonian Plain has cold winters, often made more severe with biting, freezing winds called *kosava*. Summers on the plain are dry and hot, with temperatures sometimes reaching 100 degrees Fahrenheit. The mountainous regions get much snow in winter and rains in spring, and they tend to be warm in the mountain valleys and cool in the higher elevations. Montenegro's Adriatic coastline has a mild, Mediterranean climate.

Bordering Serbia and Montenegro to the north is Hungary. To the northeast is Romania; to the southeast is Bulgaria. Due south is the former Yugoslav republic of Macedonia, and to the southwest, bordering Kosovo, is Albania. Bosnia and Herzegovina shares a border with Montenegro and much of Serbia proper, while Croatia shares an eastern boundary with the district of Vojvodina.

National Symbol

Every nation must have a flag to represent itself, but devising one for the new nation of Serbia and Montenegro has not been easy. A law that accompanied the constitutional charter establishing the new nation of Serbia and Montenegro stated that such national symbols as a flag and anthem must be created. But members of the constitutional commission disagreed about whether or not that meant that symbols of the former Yugoslavia could be reused or adapted.

The Yugoslav flag consisted of three thick parallel lines of blue, white, and red, from top to bottom. The colors are traditional pan-Slavic ones and are based on the flag of Russia, which historically has been a powerful symbol of inspiration to the Slavic people. In addition, both Serbia and Montenegro have their own republic flags, which are similar to the federal Yugoslav flag. Each has three thick horizontal stripes of red, blue, and white, from top to bottom. The only difference between the two republics' flags is the middle stripe. On Serbia's flag it is dark blue; on Montenegro's, light blue.

A Serbian heraldic expert named Dragoljub Bacović said it would be best for all people involved to try and maintain the status quo. Bacović opined, "As far as the flag is concerned, the two flags [Serbian and Montenegrin] differ only in the proportions and shades of blue, [so] it's evident that it would not be necessary [to change the flag] as it would be difficult to find a [new] flag that would correspond to logic." He added that once one considers issues aside from the logic of the flag itself, "you end up with [artsy] flags like those of Greenland or Thailand."

As of 2004, the former Yugoslav flag was being used as the official flag of the new nation of Serbia and Montenegro.

NOTE

p. xii "'As far as the flag is concerned . . .'" Jolyon Naegele, "Serbia-Montenegro: Search For New Coat of Arms, Flag Symbolic of Past Conflict," Radio Free Europe (February 10, 2003). Available on-line. URL: http://www.rferl.org/nca/features/2003/02/10022003171116.asp. Downloaded May 29, 2003.

PART I
History

1

FROM PREHISTORY
TO 1903

Long before there were people known as Serbs and Montenegrins, there were human beings residing in what is today Serbia and Montenegro. At least 3,500 years ago, perhaps even longer, an ancient civilization living there made pottery, smelted copper, and raised food along the banks of the rivers known today as the Sava and the Danube. Not much else is known about these people, other than they most likely lived in early representations of what would today be known as small towns.

It is believed that around that time numbers of migratory people moved into the region from the plains of what is today Russia. Gradually, these people settled into different tribal groups and by the seventh century B.C. became well known for their work with raw iron. The most powerful of the tribes were likely the Illyrians.

The Greek Empire was just in its beginning stages then, and the people of present-day Serbia and Montenegro started a thriving trade relationship with the city-states of Greece. Then around 300 B.C. another tribal group began working its way into the area. Celts, highly regarded for their handiwork with iron, moved south where they settled in pockets including the area of present-day Belgrade.

As the Greek Empire was slowly crumbling, it was being superseded by the legendary Roman Empire. And as the third century B.C. was winding down, the Romans were stretching their empire across the Adriatic Sea.

They entered the Balkan Peninsula looking for needed resources of all kinds, from metals to agricultural produce to slaves. Seeking domination of the resource-rich Balkans, the Romans embarked on a series of battles with the Illyrians and other resident peoples. Generation after generation took part in these struggles.

Finally, in 29 B.C., Crassus, the Roman proconsul, or provincial governor, of Macedonia, conquered much of what is now eastern Serbia. Within four decades the Illyrians were completely defeated, and in the year A.D. 9 their land officially became the Roman province of Illyricum.

The Romans constructed fortresses, aqueducts, arenas, bridges, and a complex system of roads, and they established settlements. After a presence of about a century in the Balkans, the Romans began clashing with other invading tribes, such as the Goths, the Huns, the Bulgars, and the Avars. Such battles and skirmishes lasted more than 200 years, weakening Roman rule in this part of the Balkans.

In the fourth century the Romans' control of the Balkans began to dissipate. In the year 330 Roman emperor Constantine the Great (285?–337) relocated the capital of the empire from Rome to Byzantium, located on the Bosporus Strait, which connects the Black and Mediterranean Seas. People have long considered the strait as the point where Europe and Asia meet.

Constantine renamed Byzantium after himself, calling it Constantinople. Today it is the city of Istanbul, Turkey. Constantine is best remembered for converting to Christianity, which was a major factor in the spread of Christianity into Europe. That branch of Christianity, known as Orthodox Christianity, is still the primary religion in eastern Europe, from Greece to Russia.

The western lands of the Roman Empire finally collapsed in 476, while the eastern territories continued to prosper as the Byzantine Empire. Constantinople maintained marginal power over the tribes living in what is now Serbia and Montenegro, but their diversity and independent nature were so great that no central power was able to have any kind of significant control over them.

In the seventh century more tribes moved into the central Balkan Peninsula. Among these were the Slavs, who came from the region around the Carpathian Mountains, a major chain stretching across what is now Slovania, southern Poland, western Ukraine, and northeast Romania.

Tribe fought against tribe throughout the area, and the Byzantine Empire had trouble gaining the strong presence they wanted here. However, in 626, Byzantine emperor Heraclius (575?–641) joined up with two of the more powerful Slavic tribes, the Serbs and Croats, to force other tribes, such as the Bulgars and Avars, to move further east. The Croats settled closer to the Adriatic Sea, while the Serbs made their homes further inland.

Meanwhile, earlier settlers who had been pushed out of the areas occupied by the Croats and Serbs relocated to the southwest in what became Montenegro. A rugged land not suitable for agriculture and lacking in large mineral deposits, Montenegro was an area where few wanted to live. It became a home to those defeated tribes looking for a safe haven.

By the end of the seventh century, the Serbs occupied much of the central Balkans and began to develop their own social structure. People lived in a unit called a *zadruga* (a clan or extended family), led by a male relative. These *zadruge* lived in a village under the leadership of a male member of the extended family. As a body of many units, they in turn were ruled by a *župan*, equivalent to a chief, or king. There were times when groups of *župani* were consolidated under a *veliki župan*, or grand *župan*, but since the *zadruge* were based on family units, they tended to be small and fairly independent. If a grand *župan* did manage to take control of weak nearby tribes, it was usually for a short period of time. Members of the *zadruge* were prone to rebellion, and this early medieval period of Serbian history is generally considered a time of general unrest.

One instance when several *zadruge* were gathered successfully together under a grand *župan* occurred about 850. The main reason for this cohesion was self-defense. A *župan* named Vlastimir took charge of several clans of southern Serbs in order to fight a tribe called the Bulgars, who lived to the southeast of Serbia. The Bulgars had been trying to expand their tribal power into Serb-dominated land.

In order to strengthen their hand against the Bulgars, the Serbs accepted suzerainty under the Byzantine Empire. Their international policies were now controlled by the Byzantine Empire while they continued to make their own decisions regarding domestic issues.

With help from Constantinople, the Serb *župani* were able to successfully resist the encroaching Bulgars—at least for the time being. However, it also meant that the Byzantine Empire was able to exert control over the lives of the Serbs. The biggest effect of this influence concerned religion.

In probably the early 860s, Byzantine emperor Michael III (836–867) took advantage of his power to proselytize. He sent two brothers named Cyril (827–869) and Methodius (826–885) from the town of Thessalonica in present-day Greece to preach Christianity to all the southern Slavs. To make conversion easier, Cyril invented his own alphabet to aid communications with the Slavs. Cyril based the alphabet upon his native Greek, but he adapted it to the Slavs' speech patterns. Named after its inventor, the alphabet became known as Cyrillic. Through this new alphabet, the brothers were successful in converting sizable numbers of Serbs to Orthodox Christianity. It also served to unite the Serbs in their ethnicity and separate them from other southern Slavs, such as the Croats and Slovenes.

In some ways the Serbs were similar to their southern Slavic neighbors, such as the Bosnians and Croats. They were often subservient to bigger and more powerful groups. While the Croats were often under the thumb of Hungary and Venice, the Serbs were constantly threatened by the Bulgars and the Byzantine rulers. During the end of the 800s and the early 900s, Serb *župani* were in nearly constant conflict with the Bulgars.

A Bulgar emperor named Simeon, in power from 893 to 927, extended his dominion into much of eastern Serbia. The Serb *župani*, then allied with Byzantine emperor Caslav (927–960), were able to take back much of their lost territory from Simeon's weak successors in the mid- and late 900s. The 11th century was a time of constant civil war between the different *župani* and the Byzantine Empire. The Bulgars were conquered by the Byzantines in 1018 and at this time were not a major factor in the Serbs' lives.

The *župani* were divided into two political groups: the west, known as Zeta (and at different times, Dioclea), in what is present-day Montenegro and Herzegovina, and the east, called Raška, centered around the modern Serbian city of Novi Pazar. Because Raška was closer to Constantinople, it was vulnerable to Byzantine armies. In more distant Zeta, the various *župani* were able to stay more independent. A number of *župani* in Zeta were united around 1042 by Serb prince Vojislav. His son Michael (r. 1051–81) extended his kingdom to include Raška, thanks in large part to a grant he received from Pope Gregory VII in 1077. Even though the Serbs were mainly Orthodox Christians, they did not hesitate to maintain good relations with the Catholic Church in Rome. In the late 1000s, Michael's son Bodin (1081–c. 1101) enlarged the Serb kingdom yet again, but after his death in 1101 civil war among the *župani* broke out, and the kingdom all but disintegrated. It would take a strong leader to rebuild any kind of sizable unified Serb entity.

Such a commanding force took power in, depending on the source, either 1169 or 1170, and his name was Stefan Nemanja (1113–1200). Named grand *župan* of Raška, Stefan Nemanja was in one regard lucky to be in the right place at the right time. Byzantine emperor Manuel died in 1180, and confusion reigned in Constantinople over a successor. Stefan Nemanja took advantage of that confusion to expand his territory. By 1186 he had united Raška and Zeta. He used his control to educate, effectively govern, and mobilize the Serbs as an ethnically based state, in large part due to his support of the construction of monasteries.

He was also the first member of a political dynasty that would lead the Serbs for roughly two centuries. His middle son, Stefan Prvovenčani (Stefan "the first crowned"; 1176–1227) succeeded him in 1217. Stefan Prvovenčani solidified his authority when he was given the title of king by Pope Honorius III that year. Stefan Nemanja's oldest son, Vukan, was around the same time declared ruler of the region of Zeta. Meanwhile, Stefan Nemanja's youngest son, Rastko, became a monk and changed his name to Sava (1169–1236?).

Sava, is today credited with making Serbia a mainly Orthodox Christian country. He severed ties with the Catholic Church, preached Orthodoxy, and helped suppress an offshoot of Catholicism called bogomilism, considered a dualist religion. Bogomils rejected the Catholic teaching that the world is inherently evil and believed that there are two gods, one of evil and one of good. Bogomilism took hold in Bosnia, but, thanks in large part to the efforts of Sava, was permanently suppressed among the Serbs.

By the late 1100s, the Byzantine Empire was weakening greatly; by the early 1200s, it was on its last legs. The Bulgarians took advantage of that vacuum and expanded westward into the town of Skopje, on the Vardar River, and Ohrid, both in present-day Montenegro, south of Serbia. But medieval Serbia kept growing more powerful under strong kings like Stefan Prvovenčani successors, Stefan Uroš II (1253–1321) and Stefan Uroš III (1278–1331). With that power behind them, the Serbs in the first half of the 13th century expanded south and wrested Skopje, Prilep, and other Montenegrin towns from the Bulgarians. Then in 1330 Stefan

---

SAINT SAVA OF SERBIA

Usually depicted as a sad-eyed man with dark hair and a long, dark beard, Saint Sava, is regarded by Serb Orthodox followers as an enlightened individual of great wisdom. At just 17, this youngest son of grand *župan* Stefan Nemanja journeyed to a monastery atop Greece's Mount Athos, a holy site to Orthodox Christians. Like the other resident monks, Sava lived an austere life, praying to God, reading holy books, and fasting regularly.

His father was not happy that his son had run away from home. He sent a battalion of soldiers to find him and bring him back. At the same time, Stefan Nemanja sent an ultimatum to the ruler of the Greek province in which Mount Athos is located: His son must be returned or he would go to war against Greece. Since the soldiers had been commanded not to let the boy out of their sight, they found it necessary to be present at an evening service. During the service, they became intoxicated on wine and fell asleep, oblivious to the fact that Sava was receiving the tonsure, or taking part in the official ceremony in which part of his head is shaved as an important symbolic step in becoming part of the monastic order. Sava then sent his shaved hair, nonreligious clothing, and a letter to his parents asking them to accept his chosen way of life, which they did.

In fact, the father followed the son's lead, ultimately moving to Mount Athos, becoming a monk and taking the name Simeon. After

---

Uroš III's armies defeated the Bulgarians in what is today the Bulgarian resort town of Kjustendil, not far from the Serbia-Bulgaria border.

The Serbs tried also to expand their kingdom to the north but, except for a few spotty victories, were never able to grab control of land held by the Magyars, present-day Hungarians. They had similar problems in attempting to expand to the west into Bosnia. For a while Stefan Uroš III held control of the principality of Hum, today Herzegovina, but lost it to the Bosnians in 1325.

While they never expanded as far as they wished, in the 14th century the Serbs enjoyed military and economic supremacy over much of the interior Balkans. An economic revolution based on agriculture and mining was bursting out of Serbian-controlled lands. Throughout the Balkans,

his father's death, Sava brought his father's remains back to his homeland and took up residence at a monastery his father had helped build, the Monastery of Studenica. In time Sava became the superior of the monastery, and he was responsible for training and teaching Serbian monks. He also advised his brother, the king Stefan Prvovenčani.

When Sava returned to Serbia, his nation's bishops and archbishops were Greeks, considered by the Serbs to be outsiders. Wanting to strengthen Serb identity, Sava believed it was important for Serbia to be under the jurisdiction of Serb bishops. He traveled to the city of Nicea in Asia Minor, present-day Turkey, where the Greek king and patriarch lived, and requested the appointment of a Serbian bishop. The request was granted, and in 1219 Sava was given the title of the first Serbian archbishop. Upon returning home, Sava got together with his brother, the king, and appointed Serbs as bishops throughout his country. He oversaw the construction of churches and monasteries where Serbian children were taught to read and write.

After his death, Sava was buried at the Serbian Monastery of Mileševo. His gravesite became a shrine to Serbs. The Turks, who were to rule Serbia in the 16th century, hoped to erase Sava from the Serbs' collective memory; in 1594 they dug up Sava's body and burned it. The Serbs have never forgotten St. Sava, and his memory is the focus of a Serb religious holiday, St. Sava's Day, celebrated on January 27. Special services take place, and children are awarded with gifts.

Serbia was known for its flour production. Other products resulting from mass cultivation in Serbia included wine, hemp, and flax. Livestock, especially pigs and cattle, were raised in profusion as well. The Serbian political capital was moved from the older city of Raška to bustling Skopje, which had already developed into the Serbs' agricultural capital.

Yet Serbia's booming economy was not based on agriculture alone. Copper, tin, gold, and silver mines had been exploited in Roman times but had been laying dormant for centuries. The Serbs reopened them, and before long they were minting their own coins and crafting metal luxury goods. They had superb trade relations with regional governments, especially Italy and the independent merchant republic of Ragusa, today the Croatian city of Dubrovnik.

Stefan Dušan

However, Serbia had yet to reach either its economic or political peak when Stefan Dušan (1309–55) became king in 1331. Stefan Dušan was determined to make a strong Serbia even stronger. He recruited immigrant Saxons, tribal members from present-day Germany, and Italians to work Serbia's many mines. Old Roman roads were dusted off and traversed by traders, especially from Ragusa, looking for a wide range of Serbian

THE BATTLE OF KOSOVO POLJE

The Battle of Kosovo Polje is one of the defining events in Balkan, especially Serbian, history. Serbs have spoken for centuries of the occurrence with the same reverence in which Americans discuss the bombing of Pearl Harbor and the terrorist attacks of September 11, 2001. It is seen as one of the bleakest events in Serbian history, but it is also evoked today to galvanize Serb identity.

The facts of what really happened that June day in Europe have vanished into the ether. According to Serb tradition, Kosovo Polje is the dividing line separating the period of Serbian power from the dark centuries of Turkish oppression. That is not entirely true, since Serb power had diminished greatly after Stefan Dušan's death 34 years earlier and a Serb state existed in a weaker form for about 70 years after the battle.

Indeed, what happened at the actual Battle of Kosovo Polje itself is not really known. There were no cameras in 1389 to record the action. There were no reporters on the scene, and no mass telecommunications existed. As such, the narrative of the events has been twisted and embellished from generation to generation. Amazingly, the battle, today regarded as a crushing defeat of the Serbs, was not depicted that way in its time.

The first written account of the battle was made 12 days after the fighting ended by a Russian monk living in Ottoman-controlled land. He made no mention of who won or lost, but he did note that Ottoman sultan Murad (1326?–89) died in the fighting. On August 1, 1389, Bosnian king Tvrtko wrote letters to the governments of Dalmatia and Florence, speaking glowingly of the battle, as if it were a Slavic victory. Scholars today are certain that in addition to the sultan, Serb leader Prince Lazar Hrebeljanović died in battle, too. It is believed by

goods, including leather, timber, and wine. Stefan Dušan's plan was to use all this wealth to expand to the southeast.

Through military might and political skill, by 1335 Stefan Dušan occupied all of present-day Macedonia and parts of what are today Greece and Bulgaria. The rest of Bulgaria, while technically not a territory of Serbia, was basically a dependency of the Nemanja family. To the southwest Serbia occupied all of modern-day Albania, and to the northwest, Ragusa. In a glorious ceremony in the Serbian capital city of Skopje on Easter Day 1346,

historians that the immediate result of the battle was not a crushing Serb defeat but, instead, the beginning of events leading to an ultimate Serb downfall. What most likely happened after the battle was an intense reorganization of power for both the Serbs and Turks. With the Turks more powerful in soldiers and supplies, the Serbs soon submitted to the Turks' authority.

One of Serbia's best-known poets, Vuk Karadžić (1787–1864), told the tale of the battle in a saga titled *Lazar's Choice: The Empire of Heaven*. In the epic poem, a heroic Lazar receives a message from the Mother of God in the form of a hawk holding a swallow. Lazar is then offered a choice. A portion of the poem reads:

'Lazar, glorious Emperor,
which is the empire of your choice?
Is it the empire of heaven?
Is it the empire of the earth?
If it is the empire of the earth,
saddle horses and tighten girth-straps,
and, fighting-men, buckle on swords,
attack the Turks,
and all the Turkish army shall die.
But if the empire of heaven
weave a church on Kosovo,
built its foundation not with marble stones,
build it with pure silk and with crimson cloth,
take the Sacrament, marshal the men,
they shall all die,
and you shall die among them as they die.' . . .
And the emperor chose the empire of heaven
above the empire of the earth.

THE OTTOMAN EMPIRE

The peak years of the Ottoman Empire, mainly the 16th and 17th centuries, are regarded as among the greatest flowerings of human art, culture, and governmental structures. During that time the noted empire stretched from southwestern Europe to present-day Iran, Saudi Arabia, and northern Africa. It was probably the most influential Muslim empire in history.

The Ottoman Turks were ruled by a single leader, called a sultan, who had absolute power. His main function was to guarantee justice, known in Arabic as àdala, especially among the peasant class. Politically and religiously, the Ottoman model of the just leader was King Solomon from the Old Testament of the Bible. The most powerful and most highly regarded Ottoman sultan during the empire was Suleiman I (1494?–1566), also known as Suleiman the Magnificent and the Lawmaker, who ruled from 1520 until his death. The name Suleiman is an Arabic form of Solomon.

To ensure justice, the sultan was mandated to tour the empire incognito, in order to objectively observe regional civil servants and judges. If he saw an injustice being committed, he was required to overturn it, and in some ways the Ottoman judicial system was fairer than that of Christian Europe. In one instance, in 1521, an Ottoman court sentenced to death a man named Molla Kabiz for publicly declaring the spiritual superiority of Jesus over Muhammed. Sultan Suleiman overturned the verdict, saying that arguments made in court against Molla did not disprove his statement. At about the same time, Protestant Reformation leader Martin Luther was sentenced to death in Germany for challenging the supreme authority of the Catholic Church. Luther's supporters hid him in a castle to spare him from death.

Stefan Dušan was crowned with a new title: emperor of the Serbs and Greeks. As the Serbian empire expanded, so did Stefan Dušan's title. He would soon become emperor and autocrat of the Serbs and Greeks, the Bulgarians and Albanians.

Aside from his military conquests, Stefan Dušan is best remembered today for developing the Zakonik, or code of laws, which combined traditional Byzantine law and Serb customs. Most historians believe Ste-

In general, the Ottomans were devout Muslims who tolerated, but did not treat equally, religious minorities, such as Jews and Christians. Non-Muslims could not vote nor own property, and they had to pay taxes Muslims were not required to pay. While there was not any kind of effort made toward mass conversion to Islam, there were cases in which some non-Muslims became Muslims against their will. In a system known as *devsirme,* young non-Muslim males were taken from their families and converted in order to become servants to the Ottoman rulers. Those who did not become servants were drafted into the Ottoman army, where they became indoctrinated into the Muslim ways of belief.

In the early days of the empire, Ottoman schooling took place in mosques, or Islamic houses of worship, and was for boys only, but by the mid-1800s secular education for both boys and girls was common. Members of each religion formed a group called a *millet,* who elected a leader to represent them before the sultan.

The Ottoman Empire became wealthy mainly through trade, and some of the most frequently traveled trade routes between Europe and Asia traversed the empire. A stroll through any Ottoman marketplace from the 1400s through the 1800s would likely show for sale Asian spices, Persian silks, Chinese porcelains, and European woolens. The Ottomans also contributed much to the world of fine arts, particularly in terms of rug weaving, tile making, and a distinctive style of architecture.

The Ottoman Empire peaked in 1683, when the Turks attempted to attack Vienna but were defeated. Still, the empire survived for more than two more centuries. But its territory gradually declined as individual peoples claimed independence. Historians attribute this to weak and corrupt sultans who became detached from governmental duties. But the empire technically did not end until the modern-day Turkish republic was established in 1923.

fan Dušan's ultimate goal was to conquer storied Constantinople. The Turkish Ottoman Empire was coming into its own when Stefan Dušan was in power, and historians think a possible motive for taking Constantinople would have been to stop the Turkish Muslims from entering Christian Europe. But while he was making plans for an invasion to the southeast, likely aimed at Constantinople, Stefan Dušan died of a fever in 1355.

Stefan Dušan's son Stefan Uroš V (1332–71) took over the Serb throne, but after his father's death the many districts under Serbia's control began to assert themselves, claiming the right to self-rule or even independence. Stefan Uroš V was not the strong leader his father was, and with the Turks gaining power the inevitable happened. The Serbian empire began to disintegrate. One casualty was the district of Zeta. Led by the house of Balsa, Zeta declared its independence and became the state of Montenegro.

For a short time, some of the diverse Serb rulers were able to unify in an attempt to repel the Ottomans' advance. Whatever effort they could muster proved futile on September 26, 1371, in a battle on the Maritsa in what is today southern Bulgaria. Later that year, Stefan Uroš V died, and with him, the Nemanja dynasty—he had no son to pass his title on to. After his death, Stefan Uroš's holdings went to leaders of smaller regions of Serbia. One of those, Prince Lazar Hrebeljanović (1329–89), became his successor.

Under Lazar, the strong Turks began gobbling up more and more Serb territory. The subversion of Serbia was completed on June 15, 1389, during a now legendary event in Balkan history: the Battle of Kosovo Polje, (Field of the Blackbirds).

Under the leadership of Lazar, the Serbs combined forces with other central and eastern European armies from local regions, including Bosnia, Croatia, Hungary, and Bulgaria, to take on the steamrolling Turks. The Turks won in a decisive battle, Lazar was killed in the fighting together with many of the leading Serbian nobility, and the Serbs would never again have the power they enjoyed under the Nemanja dynasty.

In the wake of the Turks' victory, many Serbs fled their homeland. Some went north to a district of Hungary called Vojvodina. Others traveled west to Bosnia and the district of Dalmatia on the Adriatic Coast, now part of the republic of Croatia. Still others fled southwest to the mountainous state of Montenegro. Eventually, though, the Ottoman Empire would control much of those areas, too. The last Serbian stronghold, Smederevo, fell to the Turks in 1459.

While Turkish Muslim rule was not fair to Serbs, it was not brutal. The Muslim Turks tolerated the Orthodox Christians, making no effort to convert them en masse to Islam. It has been suggested that the Serbs were tolerated better under the Muslim Turks than they would have been had they been controlled by their Catholic neighbors in Hungary or Croatia.

While some of Serbia's Slav neighbors, such as Croatia and Slavonia, became independent in the 17th century, most of Serbia remained under Ottoman control until 1718. In that year the Treaty of Passarowitz was signed, following an Austrian defeat of Turkey, and a bit of northern Serbia came under the rule of Austria. However, the Serb Orthodox were treated worse under the Austrian Christians than they had been under the Turks, and many Serbs living in the newly conquered lands left to live under the Turks in the rest of Serbia. While the Turkish empire gradually weakened, there was no respite for the Serbs. The Greek Orthodox Church filled the vacuum left by the retreating Turks, but they did not treat the Serbs any better than anyone else had. During most of the 1700s, the Greek Orthodox Church dismissed Serb Orthodox clergy, replacing them with their own, and substituted Serb Orthodox rites and liturgy with those in Greek.

The lives of most of the Serbs were not good during this time, regardless of whom they lived under. Peasants were oppressed, their fields were neglected, and many had abandoned their homes. The one exception to the rule were the Serbs living in the northern district of Vojvodina. Heavily under the influence of Hungary, the Serbs of Vojvodina thrived through trade with Hungary and other lands of the mighty Hapsburg Empire.

Montenegro

Montenegro would experience trouble with the Ottoman Empire as well. After the last male heir of the Balsa dynasty died in 1455, a new leader named Stefan Crnojević (1427–65) took over the land, by then called Montenegro. He established his political capital in the community of Žabljak, on the northeastern shore of Lake Scutari in southwestern Montenegro. He was succeeded by a member of the Crnojević family who would become a legend in Montenegrin history: Ivan the Black.

By the late 1400s, the Ottoman Turks had conquered much of the Balkans, including Bosnia and Herzegovina, and Ivan was wise enough to know that the lakeside capital of Žabljak was vulnerable. So he withdrew from Žabljak and headed to less accessible mountainous country to the northwest. There he established a new governmental seat in the town of Cetinje. Thanks in large part to his remote capital, Ivan successfully fought off the Turks; today he is fondly remembered as the leader who saved Montenegro from Ottoman control.

However, the site of Cetinje was also a curse. An inland town with little arable land, it lacked easy access to trade and had poor growing soil. The capital of Montenegro was thus destined to struggle economically.

Other feats of Ivan included bringing the first printing press to the country in 1493 and establishing a monastery in Cetinje, which became a bishopric, or a bishop's diocese. When Ivan's last direct heir died in 1516, these same bishops, known as *vladikas*, began to rule over Montenegro and changed the country from civil leadership to a theocracy. Unlike Montenegro's previous rulers, who ascended to the leadership position based on the family name, the *vladikas* were elected by regional assemblies.

Legendary Montenegrin ruler Ivan the Black established the first monastery in Cetinje in the late 1400s. This picture of the Cetinje Monastery was probably taken between 1890 and 1900. (Courtesy Library of Congress)

For the next couple of centuries, Montenegro was in an almost constant state of war with the Ottomans. Three times—in 1623, 1687, and 1712—Cetinje was actually captured by the Turks. But each time the Turks withdrew shortly afterwards. Some historians cite the Montenegrins' stubborn nature and their strong ties with the mighty empire of Venice as reasons for the inability of the Turks to gain permanent control of Montenegro. But nearly all historians think that the tough terrain of Montenegro was a factor as well. A common saying regarding Montenegro's history is, "A small army is beaten, a large one dies of starvation."

The form of selecting a leader of Montenegro changed drastically when Danilo Petrović (1670?–1737) of Njegoš was elected *vladika* in 1696. Known as Danilo I, this new *vladika* was permitted to name his own successor. Naturally, his first choice was a family member. Since bishops are required to be celibate, Danilo I chose his nephew, Sava, to succeed him at his death. During his reign, Danilo I's greatest accomplishment was establishing diplomatic ties with a strong ally, Russia, who was also involved in an ongoing struggle against the Turks. The empire of Venice was declining in power, and the Russians under Czar Peter the Great gave subsidies to the Montenegrins to help build their country.

When Danilo died in 1737, Sava, as scheduled, became *vladika*, but he turned out to be as weak a leader as his uncle was strong. Much of the time he allowed others, including his cousin Vasilije and an eccentric adventurer named Stefan Mali, to be at the helm. Tribal differences between Montenegrins rose to the surface, and skirmishes were common, with leadership doing nothing to stop violent disputes. But upon Sava's death in 1782, his nephew Peter I (r. 1782–1830) became *vladika*. Like Danilo I, Peter I was an intelligent and effective leader.

Thanks to Peter's wisdom, most disputes between the varying clans ended, and Montenegro became more or less a united state. In 1798 Peter established the Montenegrin code of laws, and the next year he was able to get Ottoman leadership to formally recognize the independence of Montenegro. In addition, the Turks declared that the Montenegrins had never been their subjects. Around the same time, a battle against the Turks resulted in Montenegro formally acquiring a land to the northeast known as the Brda.

Gains for Serbia

A war broke out in 1787 between the Austrians, who were allied with the Russians, and the Turks. The Austrians called on the Serbs to fight with them against their longtime occupiers, the Turks. The Serbs answered that call, and after the Treaties of Sistova and Jassy were signed in 1791 and 1792, the Austrians rewarded the Serbs with a written defense of their civil rights. But the Turks soon returned, and with them came unfair leadership and attacks against the Serbs.

By now, many of the Serbs had had enough. It took a pig trader with coal-black hair, George Petrović (1760–1817) to encourage and impassion his compatriots. Known as Karageorge (or Karadjordje; Black George), because of his hair, he called for a *skupština* (an assembly) in April 1805 to gather a list of demands for local autonomy, which would be presented to the sultan. These were rejected, and what began as a peaceful request turned into an armed rebellion that lasted several years.

Things looked promising for the Serbs, especially after 1808, when the Russians entered the rebellion on the Serbs' side. But by 1812 the Russians withdrew from Serbia to defend their homeland against French emperor Napoleon. The Treaty of Bucharest was negotiated between the Turks and the Russians in May 1812. Part of the treaty called for Serbian autonomy, but it was never enforced. Fearing retribution from the Turks, Karageorge fled into the Serb-populated area of Hungary in 1813.

A second rebellion ensued, under a man of peasant stock named Miloš Obrenović (1780–1860), in April 1815. Since Napoleon had by now fallen, Russia was free to help their Serb neighbors. With the Russians behind them, the Serbs were able to negotiate with the Turks from a position of some strength. As a result of the treaty, Serbia officially continued as a Turkish principality, but it was basically operated as an independent state under Miloš Obrenović.

Karageorge returned in June 1817 and was soon murdered. He had never gotten along well with Obrenović, and Karageorge's family suspected the Obrenović family had something to do with his assassination. A blood feud between the two families had begun and would continue for the rest of the century.

Finally, in 1830, the Ottomans granted the Serb principality complete autonomy. The Serbian Orthodox Church was given full independent status, and Miloš Obrenović was recognized as the hereditary prince.

Gains for Montenegro

Peter I's nephew, Peter II (1813–51), ascended to the position of *vladika* after the death of his uncle in 1830. He continued the good work of his namesake, keeping rebellious factions in order, and he further centralized the government by establishing a permanent senate in Cetinje in 1831. Peter added a bit of culture to his post: He was a talented poet, best known for an epic poem called *The Mountain Wreath,* which told the tale of the Montenegrins' conflicts with the Turks.

Those were not empty words. A short war with Turkey broke out again in 1832 over the refusal of the Montenegrins to accept Turkish suzerainty. Montenegro won the war, but tensions between Montenegro and Turkey continued to mount.

Tired of centralization, the people of a district called Crnička, as well some in Brda, tried seceding from Montenegro. After a short civil war in 1847 they were reunited. Peter died in 1851, and his successor Danilo II (1826–60) established a change in governmental procedure. Since he wished to marry, Danilo II separated the religious and secular offices of Montenegrin leadership. The office of *vladika* was no more. Danilo II took the title of *gospodar* (prince). After he was assassinated by a Montenegrin rebel in 1860, his nephew Nicholas I (1841–1921) took the throne.

As was typical by now, disputes with Turkey continued, and borders changed. As a result of one war and the subsequent Treaty of San Stefano, signed on March 3, 1878, and Treaty of Berlin, signed on July 13, 1878, Montenegro was given the town of Bar on the Adriatic Sea and thus officially had a seaport. In the latter part of the 19th century, Nicholas helped modernize his land by building roads and making it more conducive for agriculture, especially crops such as tobacco and grapes.

The End of an Era in Serbia

Serbian leadership for the rest of the century alternated between the rival Karageorge and Obrenović families. The last Turkish troops withdrew from Serbia in 1867 under Prince Michael, younger son of Miloš. However, war broke out again in the region in 1875 when Bosnia rebelled

The Obrenović dynasty lasted for nearly a century. This monument in Belgrade depicts Prince Michael of the Obrenović family. (Courtesy Library of Congress)

against their Turkish landlords. To defend their Slavic neighbors, Serbia and Montenegro declared war on Turkey, and they were joined again by the Russians in 1877. The Treaty of Berlin in July 1878, which ended the war, carved up the Balkan map, adding territory from what had been Bulgaria to Serbia and Montenegro. Then, in 1881, King Milan (1854–1901) of the Obrenović family made a secret pact with Austria. The primary condition was this: Serbia would be given excellent trade deals if it promised to stay out of any conflicts between Austria and Bosnia and Herzegovina. King Milan then tried to grab land from Bulgaria by attacking the country to the east. That campaign was a failure and, along with personal scandals, cause for Milan to abdicate the throne in 1889. His son, Alexander (1876–1903), took Milan's spot on the throne, but unrest in Serbia due to interparty disagreements and corruption did not abate. The kingdom was a financial mess, and there was a feeling of national anger. To add to the instability, Alexander married his unpopular mistress, Draga Mašin (1866–1903) in 1900. On June 10, 1903, Alexander and Draga were assassinated in the palace in Belgrade by his own officers. The Obrenović dynasty had ended.

NOTES

p. 11 "'Lazar, glorious emperor . . .'" Tim Judah, *The Serbs: History, Myth & The Destruction of Yugoslavia*. New Haven, Conn.: Yale University Press, 1997, pp. 34–35.

pp. 14–15 "It has been suggested . . ." Stephen Clissold, *A Short History of Yugoslavia: From Early Times to 1966*. Cambridge, England: The University Press, 1966, p. 105.

p. 17 "'A small army is beaten . . .'" Dusan Batakovic, History of Serbia and Montenegro. Available on-line. URL: http://www.kosovo.com/serhist.html. Downloaded March 28, 2003.

2

1903 THROUGH THE DEATH OF TITO

The year 1903 began on a high note, and for half a decade things looked promising for the people of these long-troubled lands. In search of a new leader, the Serbian *skupština* (assembly) offered the position of king to another member of the Karageorge family, Peter Karageorgević, the son of a former king who had been living in exile in Geneva, Switzerland. Peter accepted the offer and proved himself a skilled monarch. He liberalized some of Serbia's tough laws, making Serbia a constitutional monarchy and limiting the king's power. Through his tactful diplomacy Peter also improved trade and solidified his nation's economy.

Yet, because of fights over tariffs with mighty Austria-Hungary, the Serbs were unable to fully exploit the potential trade. The leaders of this landlocked nation believed a seaport on the Adriatic was mandatory for future economic growth, and a popular chant at the time was "Serbia must expand or die."

But where should that Serb-controlled seaport be? Many Serbs wanted to go into Bosnia and Herzegovina. Others favored Macedonia to the south, still under the control of the remnants of the Ottoman Empire. Montenegro, unfortunately, was out of the question. Peter thought an expansion could be made by negotiation, but he and Montenegrin prince Nicholas, who was ruling his small nation as a virtual dictator, were not getting along well.

That drive for a seaport, as well as Serbia's good spirits, came to a crashing halt in 1908. The Austrian-Hungarian Empire officially annexed Bosnia and Herzegovina. Serbs were outraged and called for war against Austria-Hungary. Russia sided with its fellow Orthodox compatriots. However, Austria-Hungary was allied with strong Germany, and neither Russia nor Serbia wanted a conflict with the combined forces of those two military powerhouses.

So Serbia turned their desires for a seaport to Macedonia. The Turks, embroiled in a military conflict with Italy, were weak and distracted. Thanks to Peter's political skills, in 1911 and 1912, Serbia was able to form friendly alliances with former nemeses Bulgaria and Greece. He also was able to finally manage an alliance with Nicholas of Montenegro. As a result of these agreements, the four nations gelled together as one group, known as the Balkan League, and they had one goal: to remove the Turks from Macedonia.

On March 13, 1912, Serbia and Bulgaria signed a treaty spelling out agreements for the division of Macedonia among Serbia and Bulgaria. But it was Montenegro, of all nations, that was the first to officially declare war on Turkey, on October 8, 1912. Many observers were stunned by how quickly the members of the Balkan League ran roughshod over Turkey in a conflict known as the First Balkan War. The Treaty of London, signed on May 30, 1913, carved up Turkey's former possessions in southeastern Europe.

The peace lasted for an eye blink. Bulgaria felt it was treated unfairly by being given what it thought was a too small share of Macedonia. In June 1913 Bulgaria commenced military hostilities against Serbia and Greece, and a second Balkan War had begun. The war lasted a matter of weeks as Serbia, together with Greece and Montenegro, beat back the Bulgarians. In the Treaty of Bucharest, signed in August 1913, Serbia, Montenegro, and Greece were all awarded greater territory. A tiny independent territory called Novi Pazar, located between Serbia and Montenegro, was divided between the two nations, giving them a common border. Much of northern and central Macedonia went to Serbia, while Greece was awarded other Macedonian lands, including those on the coast.

Reactions were disparate. Serbs and Montenegrins were thrilled, and they began to envision some kind of South Slav unity based spiritually, if not politically, in the Serb capital of Belgrade. But Austria-Hungary saw a powerful Serbia and Montenegro as a threat that would cause nothing but trouble for its supremacy in the region.

As 1913 turned into 1914, the Balkans were a powder keg waiting for an explosion. The slightest provocation could trigger the fuse at any-time. That provocation occurred on June 28, 1914, when the heir to the Austrian-Hungarian throne, Archduke Francis Ferdinand and his wife, Sophie, made a state visit to the city of Sarajevo in Bosnia and Herze-govina, still under the thumb of Austria-Hungary. To the people of the southern Balkan states, Francis Ferdinand and his wife were symbols of Austro-Hungarian power.

A Teenager Changes World History

Before any official meetings began, the archduke and his wife were to take part in a ceremonial motorcade down Appel Quay, one of Sarajevo's main streets. Among the hordes of people waving to and cheering the visiting royalty were eight would-be assassins. They were members of an associa-tion of extreme Serbian nationalists called the Black Hand, which claimed that Bosnia and Herzegovina belonged to Serbia, not Austria-Hungary. Its leader, Dragutin Dimitrijević, was the head of military intel-ligence in the Serbian army. The Black Hand had a simple mission on that early summer day: to assassinate the archduke, thereby removing the heir apparent to the throne and crippling Austria-Hungary's spirit.

As the motorcade was in progress, one of the eight Black Hand mem-bers threw a bomb at the archduke's car. Francis Ferdinand survived the attack, but the other seven would-be assassins assumed the bomb thrower had successfully done his duty and fled the scene. Francis Ferdinand went on with his planned schedule, giving a speech at a political gathering but peppering his talk with barbs directed toward the city of Sarajevo for allowing an attempt on his life to occur.

Before leaving Sarajevo, the royal couple asked to be driven to a nearby hospital in order to offer get well wishes to injured bombing victims. On the way to the hospital, the archduke's car paused briefly in front of a gro-cery store. By coincidence, one of the would-be assassins, Gavrilo (Gabriel) Princip (1894–1918), happened to be leaving the store. Realizing that the archduke was alive, Princip grabbed a gun from his pocket and fired two shots, killing both Francis Ferdinand and Sophie.

Princip's actions caused Europe to descend into turmoil. Austria-Hungary saw the assassination as not only an attack of their future leader but on their empire. Although evidence seemed to show the assassination was the work of a band of terrorists and not the entire Serb government, the people of Austria-Hungary wanted revenge against Serbia.

Austria-Hungary immediately presented Serbia with a 10-point ultimatum and demanded a response within two days. Serbia agreed with nine of the 10 points. They refused to give Austria-Hungary permission to investigate the assassination on Serbian land. Neither side would relent, and Austria-Hungary and Serbia formally broke off relations with each other on July 25. Three days later, exactly one month after the assassination, Austria-Hungary declared war on Serbia. World War I had begun.

Europe at War

Like children witnessing a schoolyard fight, the countries of Europe almost immediately took sides. Russia vowed to support its longtime ally,

GAVRILO PRINCIP

One might think a murderer blamed for starting a world war would be a muscle-laden thug or a hardened career criminal. But Gavrilo Princip was a sickly teenager with a sallow complexion.

The son of a postman of Serb descent, Princip was born July 25, 1894, in the village of Obljaj, in southwestern Bosnia and Herzegovina. He was one of nine children, but one of just three who survived infancy. Gavrilo was a quiet and reserved boy who loved to read and excelled in school. Because of his slight size and weak body, Gavrilo had a strong inferiority complex, but he tried to compensate by concentrating on his studies.

In 1911, when he was 17, Princip joined the Young Bosnia Movement, a pan-Slavic group whose goal was the unification of all the South Slavs into a single state in which South Slavs would rule themselves. But after taking an active part in an antiauthority demonstration in Sarajevo in February 1912, Princip was expelled from school. Princip then traveled permanently to Belgrade, and it is said that as soon as he

Serbia. Germany, apprehensive about what it believed to be nationalistic goals on the part of the Serbs, backed its friend, Austria-Hungary.

Germany's leader, Kaiser Wilhelm I (1859–1941), had his own nationalistic ambitions and used the pretense of the war to invade France, Switzerland, and Luxembourg on August 2. Over the next two days, Germany invaded Russia and Belgium and officially declared war on France. Right away, England entered the war in defense of Belgium and against Germany. That meant England was also on the side of Serbia, France, and Russia and against Austria-Hungary and Germany. Serbia, England, and their allies were called the Entente Powers or the Allies. Austria-Hungary, Germany, and their allies were known collectively as the Central Powers.

Powerful Austria-Hungary invaded smaller Serbia, but the Serbs were able to repel them. However, in the winter of 1914–15 a typhus epidemic swept through Serbia, severely weakening the ranks of its armed forces. Then, in October 1915, German field marshal August von Mackensen attacked Serbia from the west while at the same time Bulgaria launched an offensive from the east. Because of its depleted forces, Serbia could not defend itself against a two-pronged offensive attack. Much of the Serbian military retreated west across Albania to the Adriatic coast. The rest of

crossed the border, this young man of Serb descent but Bosnian birth bent down and kissed the soil of Serbia. He tried enlisting in the Serb army, but was turned down because of his size and feeble condition. World War I historians believe that this rejection made him determined to do something brave to prove wrong all those who said he was too weak to be a fighter.

Princip stayed active in radical politics, and two years later he was given his chance to prove himself. Serbian major Vojislav Tankosić, head of a guerilla unit in the Serb army that had rejected Princip for active duty in 1912, recruited Princip to be part of the plot to assassinate Archduke Francis Ferdinand and his wife in June 1914. After the shots were fired, Princip tried to commit suicide by shooting himself, only to have the gun knocked out of his hand by a bystander. He tried suicide again by swallowing cyanide, but he gagged and vomited it up.

Princip was captured and tried in a Sarajevo court in 1915. Found guilty, Princip was spared the death sentence because of his young age. Instead, he was sentenced to 20 years in prison. The sentence mattered little, since Princip died of tuberculosis in prison in 1918.

Serbia's armed forces and its government leaders were rescued by the navies of England and France and were taken to safety on the Greek island of Corfu.

The war deadlocked for the next year and a half, but the exiled leaders of Serbia did not simply languish on Corfu. First, Serb troops joined forces with those of Greece in November 1916 to fight the Bulgarian troops occupying Macedonia. Bloody fighting ensued, with the Bulgarians surrendering two weeks later. The fall of the Macedonian front is regarded as the first chink in the armor of the Central Powers' war machine.

Serbia's leaders also began making plans for the South Slavs after the war. At first the Serbs' goals involved the best way to reestablish their state once the war was over. Serbia's prime minister Nikola Pašić (1845–1926) hoped that Serbia's gains as a result of the 1913 Treaty of Bucharest would be validated. At best, Pašić wished his nation might even add to those territories.

But it was not to be. Serbia's strongest ally, Russia, was too bogged down with its own war-related problems, from food shortages to political

Serbia's King Peter was a skilled leader but could do little to help his depleted army fight Austria-Hungary, Germany, and Bulgaria in World War I. He is at the far left watching his troops in action during the war. (Courtesy Free Library of Philadelphia)

upheaval, to be of much support to Serbia. Croatia's diplomat Ante Trumbić, also living in exile on Corfu, was the other chief negotiator concerning the southern Slavs' postwar plans. Pašić, Trumbić, and exiled leaders from Montenegro, and Slovenia all met on Corfu in July 1917. Although Pašić feared living in a nation in which Serbs were outnumbered by Slavs of other nationalities, he had no choice but to compromise. On July 27, 1917, an agreement called the Corfu Declaration was reached.

The foremost parts of the Corfu Declaration were as follows:

1. The new pan-South Slav country would be a parliamentary monarchy under Serb leadership;
2. There would be local autonomy for specific ethnic groups based on social and economic conditions, and the specifics would be worked out at a later date; and
3. A national assembly would meet and adopt a constitution with terms agreed to by a majority.

Pašić hoped the constitutional assembly would declare that the new nation was centralized under a Serb-dominated government. That would counter the fact that the Serbs were outnumbered by other Slav peoples.

The United States had entered the war on the side of the Entente Powers in April 1917, and over the course of the next year and a half the war began to wind down. With the war's conclusion in mind, United States president Woodrow Wilson presented on January 8, 1918, a peace plan he called the Fourteen Points. The 11th point declared that Austria-Hungary and Germany must vacate Serbia and that Serbia be accorded free and secure access to the sea. In September 1918 the Entente powers swept Austria-Hungary and Germany out of Serbia, and it was obvious that the end of the war was close. A peace treaty was signed on November 11, 1918, at Versailles, near Paris, France.

Decisions by the Balkan peoples regarding unification would have to be made soon. On November 26, Vojvodina, an autonomous district of northern Serbia along the Hungarian border, announced that it would join the South Slav union. While the Croats were gun-shy about becoming part of a Serb-dominated centralized state, they agreed it was the smartest thing to do in their situation. There was potential for growth and prosperity to be gained from joining forces with the wealthier and more cosmopolitan Serbia.

Montenegro, meanwhile, took advantage of the war's end to peacefully and successfully rebel against the remnants of Austria-Hungary's leadership. In November 1918 the assembly in Cetinje deposed King Nicholas and his dynasty, then formally announced its membership as part of the Serbian state.

NIKOLA PAŠIĆ

Although he looked like a grandfather—with a thin face and a long, gray, flowing beard—Nikola Pašić survived death sentences and years in exile to become the most noted Serbian statesman for the last 10 years of the 19th and first 20 years of the 20th centuries. Born in the town of Zaječar, Serbia, near the border with Bulgaria, Pašić became involved with radical politics at an early age and was elected to the *skupština* at the age of 33 in 1878.

In 1881 Pašić founded Serbia's radical party and just two years later was sentenced to death for conspiring to kill Serbia's King Milan. Pašić survived by escaping his country and living in exile in Austria until 1888. He took a more active role in Serbian politics in 1891, when he formed his first ministry, but in 1899 he became a political prisoner, when he became involved in a heated and public dispute with King Alexander of the Obrenović dynasty and was sent to jail.

In Balkan politics circumstances change often, and from 1903 until 1918 he served as Serbia's prime minister, with the exception of a short period in 1908 when he was unpopular and temporarily removed from office. In office during both the Balkan Wars and World War I, Pašić continually found himself in controversial situations. He was in constant disagreement with the Serbian military, which longed for a Greater Serbia, yet he supported the land grabs in 1912 and 1913 during the Balkan Wars. After the assassination of Archduke Francis Ferdinand, Pašić was linked to the radical Black Hand conspirators. While most historians believe a connection between Pašić and the Black Hand is unlikely, the issue has been grist for continual debate.

Birth of a Kingdom

On December 1, 1918, Serb crown prince Alexander (1888–1934) proclaimed the new Kingdom of Serbs, Croats, and Slovenes under his leadership. The capital of the kingdom, to the disappointment of the Croats, was declared to be Belgrade.

Yet differences between the many ethnic groups in the new kingdom made it a disaster waiting to happen. From the beginning, ethnic, cultural,

Following the Austro-Hungarian invasion of Serbia in 1915 and the subsequent exile of the Serbian government to Corfu, Pašić again found himself in disagreement with Serb leadership over a Greater Serbia. This time Pašić's nemesis was King Alexander, who supported a bigger Serbia over Pašić's objections. But when Pašić began negotiations with Croatia's Ante Trumbić over the South Slavs' future following the end of World War I, he found himself on the other side of the issue, favoring a strong, spacious Serbia, as opposed to a South Slav federation, but not to the extent that the king envisioned.

Following the establishment of the Kingdom of Serbs, Croats, and Slovenes on December 1, 1918, Pašić lost his role as premier. Still, he represented Serbia at the postwar peace talks in Versailles, outside Paris, France. Though out of power, he was still an able politician, and he helped negotiate substantial territorial gains for the kingdom. He served twice as premier, for short stints, before his death in 1926.

Nikola Pašić was one of Serbia's most respected statesmen in the late 1800s and early 1900s. (Courtesy Library of Congress)

and religious strife led to everything but cooperation between the peoples of the new nation. The Croats, under the leadership of the Croatian Peasant Party head Stjepan Radić (1871–1928), did not shy away from presenting their discomfort about residing in a nation dominated by the Serbs, and this rivalry was a constant for much of the next decade.

Elections for delegates to a constituent assembly took place in November 1920, and members of 15 parties won seats. Croatia, under Radić, wanted the new kingdom to be a federation in which the different ethnic groups had some autonomy and there was not a strong central government; that way, the Croats would not be under domination of the Serbs. Serbia wanted just the opposite, with centralized leadership based in Serbia's capital of Belgrade. Radić's idea of a federation was defeated, and in response he boycotted the constitutional convention of 1921. The new constitution was declared on June 28, 1921, the anniversary of the Battle of Kosovo Polje in 1389. June 28 was also the holiday Vidovdan, also known as St. Vitus's Day, in honor of a third-century saint; the new set of laws thus became known as the Vidovdan Constitution.

There was a blemish on the constitutional ceremony, though. An unsuccessful assassination attempt was made on the life of the kingdom's prince regent. Then, just a month later, a young Bosnian communist shot and killed the kingdom's minister of the interior. As a direct result, the *skupština* passed a decree outlawing the Communist Party in the kingdom, and the 58 Communist members of the *skupština* were removed.

Because of four years of war, political rivalries were just one part of the new kingdom's problems. Debts needed to be paid, and the war-damaged infrastructure needed to be fixed. Even though more than 75 percent of the kingdom's residents were employed in the agriculture industry, there were shortages of just about everything. One reason stemmed from the inefficient feudalistic system of farming, which still was in effect throughout much of the nation. The new government eradicated feudalism in the kingdom by giving peasants their own land, but the parcels were so small that they were virtually useless.

While the kingdom did undergo some economic growth in the mining and textile industries, much of the kingdom remained undeveloped. Due to a lack of domestic economic output, the kingdom had to rely on foreign investment for jobs. Croatia, located closer to the nations of western Europe, was the recipient of more capital than southern Serbia, which became just one more issue for the two groups to argue about. Serb veterans who had served in World War I were especially bitter, believing that they had sacrificed greatly during the war, but were not reaping the benefits of peacetime.

By the mid-1920s, the economic situation in the kingdom was showing improvement. From 1924 to 1926, exports for the first time exceeded imports. In 1925 a railroad line between the coastal city of Split and the Croatian capital of Zagreb opened up the nation's interior to trade and convenient travel. And more and more vacationers from elsewhere came to the kingdom to enjoy the beautiful Adriatic coastline.

Tragedy in Belgrade

However, politically there was as much stress as ever between the Serbs and Croats. The tension reached a breaking point on June 20, 1928, when Punisa Račić, a police officer from Montenegro who believed strongly in Serb-Montenegrin nationalism, walked into a session of the *skupština* in Belgrade, pulled out a revolver, and shot Stepjan Radić and four other Croatian politicians. Two died at the scene. Stepjan Radić lingered for more than a month but died of his injuries on August 8, 1928.

Like Gavrilo Princip's assassination of Archduke Francis Ferdinand, this bloodbath triggered emotional and rash reactions. Representatives from Croatia demanded a stronger voice in the government, then walked out of the *skupština*, frustrated. Protesters took to the streets. A coalition of Serb-dominated parties tried to lead the country, while at the same time Croatians in Zagreb began organizing a countergovernment.

King Alexander was losing his grip on the country and decided the only way to save his frail union was to do something drastic. On January 6, 1929, he abolished the constitution of 1921 and did away with the *skupština*. He declared himself absolute ruler and became a virtual dictator, canceling civil liberties. In order to ease the boiling ethnic tensions of his kingdom, Alexander changed its name to Yugoslavia (land of the South Slavs). Furthermore, he erased the borders of the traditional republics of his kingdom, Croatia, Serbia, and Bosnia and Herzegovina. The nation was restructured into territorial provinces he called *banovinas*.

At first, these radical reforms did garner some support. Anything, Yugoslavs felt, was worth a try to calm the discord and even make government more efficient. But changing borders was not going to nec-essarily alter attitudes. The citizens lost patience with the extreme authority Alexander had given himself. Serbs, used to being the center of the government, were especially annoyed at having to share more power with the Croats and others. In one symbolic attempt to express unity, Serbs marching in a military parade on September 6, 1930, had to turn in their Serbian flags for Yugoslav flags.

On September 3, 1931, Alexander decided to forfeit some of his absolute powers. A new constitution was declared, some civil liberties were returned to the citizens, and some political parties were legally permitted to exist. Those based on ethnic background or religion, however, contin-ued to be illegal. Economics was the root of another problem. The Great Depression, which had hit America, was also felt in the rest of the world, and Yugoslavia was especially devastated. Businesses failed in huge num-bers, and foreign markets for Yugoslavia's agricultural products vanished.

Alexander spent the early 1930s trying to construct a mutual defense pact with other Balkan nations. That dream ended on October 9, 1934, when on a state visit to Marseilles, France, Alexander was assassinated by a Bulgarian agent from a fascist group known as the Ustaša.

The Ustaša was headed by a Croatian attorney named Ante Pavelič (1889–1959), and its main goal was liberation from what they considered the oppressive Serb-dominated leadership of their country. The Ustaša took its cue from the fascist leadership of Benito Mussolini (1883–1945), across the Adriatic Sea in Italy, by extolling the farmer as the keystone of the Croatian people, the family as the central unit of Croatian society, and the Catholic Church as the sacred authority. To the Serbs, the Ustaša was little more than a band of terrorists.

King Alexander had specified in his will that a triple regency take over Yugoslavia in case of his death. Technically, Alexander's son Peter was next in line for the throne, but at only 11 years old he was far too young in 1934 to rule a nation. So Alexander's cousin Prince Pavle (1893–1976) was chosen to head the regency. Pavle kept Alexander's cabinet and made overtures to the Croats by ordering a Croatian politi-cal prisoner named Vlatko Maček freed.

But he used poor judgment in naming as successive prime ministers two Serbs who became friendly with Mussolini's fascist Italy and Adolf Hitler's Nazi Germany: Milan Stojadinović (1888–1961), who served from June 1935 to February 1939, and Dragiša Cvetković (1893–1969), in office from 1939 to 1941. Stojadinović and Cvetković courted Germany primarily for economics and trade. Germany was much healthier financially than Yugoslavia and became Yugoslavia's main trading partner.

A New and Bigger War

The same year Cvetković took office, 1939, Germany invaded Poland, triggering the start of World War II. Over the next two years, Germany invaded and occupied much of Europe, including Yugoslavia's neighbors Hungary, Romania, and Bulgaria. On March 27, 1941, the Yugoslav military, fearing the influence and power of Germany's war machine, rose up and overthrew the Cvetković government, naming 17-year-old Peter II (1923–70), Alexander's son, as ruler. Knowing that Peter was ideologically opposed to Germany, Yugoslavs reacted by sweeping into the streets of Belgrade, shouting their approval of the new government, and chanting anti-German slogans.

That euphoria did not last. Only a week and a half later, the Luftwaffe, the German air force, began a bombing attack on Belgrade, killing thousands of Yugoslavs. A few days after that, German ground troops entered Yugoslavia from Nazi-occupied Romania and Bulgaria. Young King

This 1938 photo shows, from left to right, Serbia's then prime minister Milan Stojadinović, who courted support from Nazi Germany, standing with Nazi leaders Adolf Hitler (center) and Hermann Göring. (Courtesy Library of Congress)

Peter II and his staff escaped to London, and Yugoslavia humbly surrendered to the Nazis on April 17.

Germany immediately partitioned Yugoslavia into a group of puppet states. A new Croatian state, comprising not only Croatia but Bosnia and Herzegovina, was placed under the Ustaša, which had changed from an extremist organization intent on Croatian unity to a virulent group that preached racial superiority and collaborated with the Nazis. Their enemies were the Jews, Serbs, and Roma. Some Serbs were offered a choice of forced conversion or death. Others were given no such choice and were simply executed. That included Jews and Roma, whose property was confiscated and who were sent to death camps.

The Serbian state, meanwhile, was cut in size. Germany separated Serbia from the district of Vojvodina and reduced its southern territory by removing Serbia's land gains following the Balkan Wars of 1912 and 1913. Serbia, however, never caved to German ideology and remained strongly anti-Nazi. Germany made General Milan Nedić, a former minister of war, the leader of occupied Serbia. Some Serbs accepted Nedić's leadership, but the vast majority had little use for him. A few actually joined forces with pro-Nazi Serbian fascist commander Dimitrije Ljotić. But most rejected Nazi leadership, and some brave Serbs openly rebelled against the Nazis.

These anti-Nazis were basically organized into two camps. One was called Četniks, or Chetniks, from the Serbian word for "detachment." The Četniks were actually several different resistance groups, whose common links were resistance to the occupying Nazis and their Croatian collaborators and an abhorrence of communism. They saw themselves as the official representatives of King Peter II's government in exile, and some thought nothing of gaining revenge against the Ustaša with brutality of their own.

The most prominent Četniks group was under the control of a former general staff officer, Colonel Draža Mihajlović. Though some Četniks openly attacked members of the Ustaša or the Nazis, Mihajlović's general strategy was not to court fights but to wait for an Allied invasion, then take part in a broad uprising.

The other anti-Nazi camp was made up of communists and known as Partisans. Their leader was Josip Broz (1892–1980), a onetime metalworker in Zagreb. Under the code name Tito, Broz used his organizational skills and charisma in the 1930s to manage what was then an underground and illegal branch of the Communist Party.

The Četniks detested communism even more than the Ustaša and Nazis, and by 1941 they began fighting the Partisans, believing that a nation under fascism was preferable to one under communism. The Partisans were headquartered in the summer of 1941 in the western Serbian town of Užice, where they took over a small arms factory and printing press to publish their opinions. By September, the Nazis had struck at their headquarters and killed thousands of civilians. The Partisans were forced to retreat into Bosnia and Herzegovina.

In Montenegro, on July 13, 1941, the Partisans and Četniks put aside their differences and successfully joined together to push out occupying Nazi-sympathizing Italian forces. Italy brought in forces from Albania to regain some lost territory. The coalition between Partisans and Četniks fell apart in 1942 as the Četniks were concerned about some of the positions hard-line Montenegrin Communist leader Milovan Djilas was espousing. Like the Četniks in Serbia, those in Montenegro began to support the fascists. The Partisans did gain back a bit of land they lost, but in the spring of 1942 a combined offensive of Četniks and Italians drove the Partisans from Montenegro. A combination of Italian and Četnik forces occupied Montenegro until the collapse of Italy in September 1943. The vacuum created by the retreating Italians in Montenegro was filled by Tito's Partisans.

In effect, the Partisans were fighting two separate wars, one against the fascists and the other against the Četniks. But by late 1942 the Četnik forces in most of Yugoslavia had weakened, and the Partisans emerged as the only real organized Yugoslav group other than the occupying Nazis and fascists.

Tito and the Partisans began calling their group the Antifascist Council for the National Liberation of Yugoslavia (in Serbo-Croatian its acronym is AVNOJ). They held two major meetings during the war, one in the Bosnian town of Bihać in November 1942, and another in the medieval Bosnian city of Jajce in November 1943.

In the meetings, AVNOJ formulated an ideology, including support of equal rights for all ethnic groups and a free enterprise economic system, and commenced making plans for post-war Yugoslavia. It was decided that Tito would be the marshal and prime minister of Yugoslavia, and King Peter would not be welcomed back until a vote on the future status of the monarchy was taken. Soon afterwards, the big three allies, the United States, the Soviet Union, and Great Britain, announced that they were formally rejecting the Četniks and giving full support to the Partisans in Yugoslavia. They dropped their support of Četnik leader Draža Mihajlović in favor of Tito.

The Partisans and the Allies, especially the Soviet Union's Red Army, battled against and wore down the Nazi stranglehold on Yugoslavia. In the spring of 1944, Tito took advantage of that weakness and sent one of his most skilled commanders, Koča Popović, on a new drive from Bosnia into Serbia. A few months later, Partisan forces under Peko Dapčević entered Serbia from Montenegro. In September 1944 Tito flew to Moscow on a secret mission. He helped organize plans for the Soviet Red Army's invasion to help liberate Yugoslavia. At the same time, he got Soviet premier Joseph Stalin (1879–1953) to promise that the Soviets would leave Yugoslavia as soon as it was secure, allowing Yugoslavia to administer its own nation. Stalin also promised free and fair elections.

The Partisans and the Soviet Union's Red Army continued to wear down the Nazis and Četniks. Belgrade was liberated late in 1944, and not long afterward King Peter surrendered his powers. Then, on May 15, 1945, Germany and the Ustaša surrendered to the Partisans. World War II in Yugoslavia was over. Roughly 1.7 million Yugoslavs, or 11 percent of the population in 1941, were dead as a result of the war. Only Poland suffered a higher mortality rate of its citizens.

A Different Yugoslavia

On March 7, 1945, Tito took office as premier of postwar Yugoslavia, a position he would hold for the rest of his long life; he would run the nation as a communist regime. Theoretically, unlike the Yugoslavia between the world wars, this Yugoslavia was meant to be a federation, and Serbia and Montenegro were established as just two of the country's six republics; the others were Slovenia, Bosnia and Herzegovina, Croatia, and Macedonia.

In an effort to reduce Serbian power, the two ethnically mixed districts of Serbia, Vojvodina in the north and Kosovo in the south, were established as autonomous provinces. Yet, while the intent might have been to make the nation a federation, in reality, the republics had little real clout. The overwhelming majority of power came out of the nation's capital, Belgrade.

At first, Tito aligned his nation with the Soviet Union. Soviet troops still occupied the Eastern European nations they had liberated and controlled them as satellites. But Soviet premier Joseph Stalin did not keep his promises, including the one about free and fair elections in any of the satellite nations.

While these satellites were regarded as communist nations, their governments did not represent pure communism. In pure communism, all businesses are owned by the community, or each specific country's citizens as a unit. Private business does not exist.

But in the Soviet Union's style of communism, all businesses were owned not by the citizens but by each nation's government. Political parties other than the Communist Party were outlawed, and persons who publicly criticized their governments were usually punished, many times severely. Soviet-style communism was officially atheistic. Religious worship was either banned or very discouraged.

In the mid-1940s, Tito became uncomfortable with Stalin's dictatorial rule. From the Soviet Union's point of view, the Yugoslavs were insubordinate. In 1948 the acrimonious relations between Stalin and Tito came to a head. Stalin kicked Yugoslavia out of the Communist Information Bureau, or Cominform, an international communist organization that existed from 1947 to 1956. In response, Yugoslavia embraced a more liberal form of communism, which would become informally known as Titoism.

Tito and Titoism

Under Titoism, the Communist Party of Yugoslavia (CPY), which became the League of Communists of Yugoslavia (LCY) after 1952, owned businesses but allowed employees of Yugoslavian factories to form workers' councils, which were permitted to hire the managers they preferred to work with and to have a say in company policies. This style became known as socialist self-management. Under Tito and the CPY, there was no collective ownership of land, as in the Soviet-dominated Eastern European communist nations. People owned the land they worked.

Yugoslavia showed significant progress economically for its first decade and a half under Tito. Industry, especially textiles and metal goods, grew and became profitable. After Tito's land reforms took effect, more and more people moved from rural areas to cities. The beaches and cities of Yugoslavia became popular tourist destinations. The nation was changing from an economic backwater dependent on a peasant-based agriculture economy to a land of active industry.

Politically, Yugoslavia found itself in a precarious situation. Many nations of the world had aligned themselves behind one of two super powers: the Soviet Union or the United States. Tito was estranged from the Soviet Union, and the United States was not going to ally itself with a communist nation, no matter how moderate. Thus Tito used his talents to align himself with what were considered nonaligned or developing countries, such as Egypt and India. In 1961 Tito hosted in Belgrade the world's first conference of nonaligned nations, and he used the occasion to denounce neocolonialism. As a result of the meeting, he gained respect for his nation, and he used it to give himself and other developing countries positions of power.

The Serbs were generally among Yugoslavia's more solidly procommunist citizens. Serbs such as Alexandar Ranković, in charge of secret police and onetime vice president, and Mijalko Todorović, head of economic affairs, exemplified the hard-line bureaucratic Serb-based school of political thought.

Montenegrins for the most part were strong advocates of a pan-Slav ideology, and they welcomed the reunification of Yugoslavia based on its historic republics. Because of their enthusiasm for Tito and his way of rebuilding the nation, many Montenegrins were for the first time given high posts in the Yugoslav government.

In the early 1960s, the once robust Yugoslav economy began to slow down. While more westernized republics, such as Croatia and Slovenia, suffered least, smaller and less westernized regions, such as Montenegro and the Kosovo, experienced hard times. Serbia proper was somewhere in the middle. Some Yugoslav government officials, including high-ranking Croat Vladimir Bakarić, urged a major overhaul of the nation's economy, including encouragement for self-management and less centralization in the federal capital in Belgrade. But Ranković insisted on maintaining the Titoist status quo.

In 1966 Ranković was accused of abusing his power, including bugging the phones of other League of Communists of Yugoslavia (LCY) members, and forced to leave his post. After Ranković's departure, Tito began

Marshal Tito was already a household name across the world when this picture showing him surrounded by supporters was taken in 1950. (Courtesy Library of Congress)

to strongly consider substantial economic reform, and he led Yugoslavia in expanding trade with the European Economic Community. Even after Ranković left office, the Serbs for the most part continued to keep their strong procommunist attitudes.

Tired of living in what they considered an unfair society, various ethnic groups in Yugoslavia took to the streets in the late 1960s in open protest. In June 1968 antigovernment riots broke out on the campus of the Workers' University of New Belgrade. Five months later, ethnic Albanians living in Kosovo demonstrated and rioted, demanding their own republic. In response, the federal government added to the Yugoslav constitution an amendment permitting Kosovo residents greater local control over social and economic issues. Serbia and Montenegro strongly objected to the amendment, fearing abuses against ethnic Serbs and Montenegrins living in Kosovo.

Slovenians and Croats also protested. Probably the most noted uprising was from young Croats who expressed pride in their ethnicity through rock music and open meetings. This Croatian movement toward reform was known by different names, such as Maspok (mass movement), but today it is remembered mainly as "Croatian Spring." Maspok lasted for more than two years until the Yugoslav police and military cracked down on the protestors in December 1971.

Tito's Twilight Years

Not long afterward, Tito deposed reformist leaders in Serbia and Vojvodina, as well as in Slovenia and Macedonia. To help put a halt to any further unrest, Tito's supporters elected him president for life in 1974. At 82 years old, Tito forged plans for the future of his beloved country after his death. Instead of a president for life, there would be a system of eight rotating presidents. The presidency would include representatives from each of the six republics, as well as from Vojvodina and Kosovo. The idea behind this was that with all republics and autonomous regions represented there would be little ground for complaints of unfairness or discrimination.

An old man in charge of a nation with a broken economic system, Tito died on May 4, 1980. Because of his decades in power and as a sign of respect, he was eulogized as a national hero and a respected international statesman. The leaders of 49 nations attended his funeral. Few, if any, could have predicted the drastic changes that were on the horizon.

NOTES
p. 23 "'Serbia must expand or die.'" Stephen Clissold, *A Short History of Yugoslavia: From Early Times to 1966*. Cambridge, England: The University Press, 1966, p. 128.

p. 26 "Although evidence seemed to show . . ." Tim Judah, *The Serbs: History, Myth & The Destruction of Yugoslavia*. New Haven, Conn.: Yale University Press, 1997, p. 97.

p. 32 "Even though more than 75 percent . . ." Glenn E. Curtis, ed., *Yugoslavia: A Country Study*. Washington, D.C.: Library of Congress, 1992, p. 32.

p. 33 "By the mid-1920s, the economic situation . . ." Clissold, p. 173.

p. 38 "Roughly 1.7 million Yugoslavs . . ." Curtis, p. 42.

p. 38 "Only Poland suffered a higher mortality rate . . ." Curtis, p. 42.

3

FROM THE DEATH OF
TITO TO THE PRESENT

For 35 years Tito had been the rope holding together the six republics and two autonomous regions of Yugoslavia. Not long after his death, the rope, slowly, then steadily, began to unravel.

Yugoslavia's economy in the early 1980s was languid. Under the Communist system, business stagnated, and inflation and unemployment grew. An economic recession in western Europe in the late 1970s resulted in unemployed Yugoslav guest workers there returning home in massive numbers, adding to the out-of-work masses in the nation. The unemployment level in the poorer areas—Macedonia, Bosnia and Herzegovina, southern Serbia, and Kosovo—stood at roughly 20 percent.

To create jobs the government found itself continually borrowing money from other nations, leading to a massive increase in Yugoslavia's national debt. In 1982 the debt was an enormous $18.5 billion, making Yugoslavia one of the most heavily indebted nations in Europe. The government had to keep borrowing money just to pay the interest.

A study to look into methods of reviving the economy was commissioned in 1981. Titled the "Long-Term Economic Stabilization Program," also known as the Krajgher Commission Report, it was released in 1983 and was highly critical of the nation's economic system. One primary conclusion of the report was that the establishment of a free market system of economics was needed. But with a huge and long-standing bureaucracy in place, the government did little to make the goals of the Krajgher Report reach fruition.

A stagnating economy was not the only problem facing Yugoslavia. Without Tito's strong hand and political skills, old ethnic rivalries began waking from their dormancy. In 1981 and 1982, ethnic Albanians in Kosovo, who comprised more than half the population of that district, took to the streets in angry protest, demanding status as not just an autonomous division but as a full republic. There were deaths and injuries, and protesters were sent to prison for their public actions, but Kosovo did not get any closer to receiving its independence.

Yugoslavia was given a huge boost economically in 1984 when Sarajevo, capital of Bosnia and Herzegovina, hosted the Winter Olympics. Athletes from 49 nations came to the ancient city to participate in the event, and that brought in millions of dollars to the money-hungry country. But that gain was short-lived, and not long after the closing ceremonies Yugoslavia's economic troubles surfaced once more. It was clear that most comfortably entrenched government officials did not even want economic reform, for fear of losing their jobs.

A Scandal Rocks the Nation

The depths of Yugoslavian economic ineptitude and corruption was made public as a result of a scandal that scratched the veneer of the financial establishment. It all started in 1987 with a fire at a warehouse that belonged to a company called Agrokomerc, headquartered in the town of Velika Kladuša, in Bosnia and Herzegovina. Agrokomerc was thought at the time to be one of the few success stories of the Yugoslav business world.

After an initial investigation of the fire, it was discovered that Agrokomerc was hardly a shining star in the business sphere in the Balkans. The company was in deep financial trouble. It was operating on 800 million dollars of unsecured loans, which meant that it did not have the hard cash to pay its employees. Further research made it clear that dozens of banks across the nation were involved in the Agrokomerc mess, as well as several members of the government. Agrokomerc, it then became apparent, was just one part of an epidemic, and many other Yugoslav businesses were being run in the same manner.

Corruption in business and government was shown to be widespread, and as a result of this far-reaching scandal, which started with a simple investigation of a fire, hundreds of Communist government officials were fired from their jobs. Bribery was widespread, with people in business paying politicians not to report dishonorable business practices.

Ethnic Unrest Again

Economic improprieties were just some of the matters tearing at the fabric of Yugoslavia at the time. On September 24, 1986, a Belgrade newspaper printed a memorandum written by anonymous members of the Serbian Academy of Sciences (SANU) stressing that they felt that the Serb community in Kosovo was in danger of being destroyed by rebellious Albanians and that Serbs in Croatia faced survival threats they had not seen since World War II. In sum, the memorandum emphasized that Serbian nationalism should be a top priority.

In April 1987 a meeting of Serb and Montenegrin officials took place at Kosovo Polje, revered site of the famous 14th-century battle against the Ottoman Turks. The principal topic was to be the alleged discrimination by the majority ethnic Albanians against the minority Serbs in Kosovo, but the biggest newsmaker of the event turned out to be an obscure Belgrade official and former business

Because of continuing protests, first secretary of the League of Communists of Serbia Ivan Stambolić, left, was let go from his job and replaced by Slobodan Milošević, right, in 1987.
(AP Photo/Matija Kokovic)

leader named Slobodan Milošević (b. 1941). Within a decade his name would be synonymous with the political monsters in 20th-century history.

Milošević gave an impassioned speech praising Serbian ethnicity. About 15,000 Serbian demonstrators had gathered in the streets to show solidarity for Kosovan Serbs, and after Milošević's speech, they became violent, clashing with the local police. Milošević called out words of support for the rioting Serbs: "No one should dare to beat you."

Those words instilled a fighting spirit in the Serbs and their close friends, the Montenegrins. Thousands of people from both republics marched in protest in Belgrade in June 1987, and civil unrest continued in both Kosovo and Vojvodina. Because of these ongoing protests and his inability to contain them, the first secretary of the League of Communists of Serbia (LCS), Ivan Stambolić, was booted from office and replaced by Milošević. After unrest in the streets continued over the next two years, Montenegro's leaders resigned under pressure in January 1989 and were replaced by Milošević sympathizers.

Milošević was elected president of the Serb republic in May 1989 and soon afterward called on Serbs to embark on a mass emigration to Kosovo in order to counterbalance the higher number of ethnic Albanians in the district. This did not sit well with Yugoslavs in the other republics, especially in Croatia and Bosnia and Herzegovina—where Serbs constituted a sizable minority—who were concerned about potential expansionist actions on Milošević's part. Meanwhile, the Republic of Croatia had its own nationalistic movement brewing, headed by a former publisher and army general named Franjo Tudjman (1922–99). Tudjman and the Croatian nationalists opined that the Serbs had too much power in the federal government.

As the Yugoslav economy continued on its downward trend workers reacted by striking against the management of several Yugoslav businesses. Labor strikes were a rarity under Tito, especially in Tito's first 15 years, when the nation was prospering. But in 1989 it was reported that roughly 1,900 separate strikes took place.

The Downfall of Communism

Similar upheavals were sweeping other Eastern European nations in 1989. The Communist Soviet satellite nations were toppling as citizens of nations from East Germany to Bulgaria demanded freedom from these dictatorships. The residents of East Berlin were among the most strident. On November 9, 1989, they took hammers and axes in hand and began tearing down the Berlin Wall, a mostly concrete barricade built in 1961 by Communist East Germany to keep East Germans from escaping into democratic West Berlin.

Almost immediately after being built, the wall became a metaphor of communist oppression. Leaders of the United States and other democratic countries publicly urged the East German government to take down the wall and allow all Berlin residents to move about in freedom. No East German government ever did so, but angry and frustrated East German citizens did on that fall day in 1989. The impromptu destruction of the wall became a much photographed event across the world.

In rapid succession, as the decade of the 1980s came to a close, one Communist satellite nation tumbled after another. Within weeks, the Communist governments of Bulgaria, Czechoslovakia, and Romania all fell. The 1990s began with a new world order.

The End of Yugoslavia

The Communist government of Yugoslavia was toppled as well, but in a more gradual manner. In 1989 the assembly of the republic of Slovenia voted to amend its constitution by adding a provision declaring its position as a sovereign state and affirming its right to secede from Yugoslavia. Realizing that this was a serious threat to Yugoslavian unity, Belgrade punished Slovenia by imposing economic sanctions on the rebellious republic.

In April and May 1990, two of the six Yugoslav republics, Slovenia and Croatia, held general elections. In Slovenia, an anti-Milošević candidate named Milan Kučan was elected president. Croatians elected nationalist and anticommunist Franjo Tudjman president, and members of Tudjman's party, the Croatian Democratic Union (HDZ), took control of Croatia's assembly, clearly indicating the Croatian voters' unhappiness with the League of Communists of Croatia (LCC).

Ethnic Serbs living in Croatia were anxious about Tudjman's nationalistic rhetoric. To pacify them, Tudjman named a Croatian Serb as vice president. But that gesture was an empty one. Croatia's Serbs, who constituted a majority in Krajina, an area in eastern Croatia, held a referendum and declared themselves a separate Serb state called the Republic of Krajina. No other countries recognized this new state.

In spite of these fractures in the nation's structure, the wheels of the federal government kept turning. In May 1990 Serbia's Borislav Jović replaced a Slovenian as Yugoslav leader under the system of rotating presidents. Serbia's anxiousness regarding the unity of the federal public was manifested in policy changes in July that year, when the Milošević government amended Serbia's constitution to end the autonomous status of Vojvodina and Kosovo. Both districts were suddenly under full control of Serbia in spite of the fact that this action was in direct violation of laws established by the federal Communist leadership of Yugoslavia. The assemblies and regional governments of both districts were broken up. Ethnic Albanians who held local public offices were fired.

The response from Kosovo was quick and angry. A group of ethnic Albanian deputies attempted to grab control of Kosovo and secede from Serbia. In September a general district-wide strike was declared to protest the firings of the ethnic Albanian officeholders. Those who made efforts to reorganize the autonomous government of Kosovo were arrested and charged with belonging to an illegal separatist organization.

Late in 1990 elections were held in the other four Yugoslav republics. In two of them, Bosnia and Herzegovina and Macedonia, anticommunist and pronationalist parties were most successful. In Serbia Milošević was reelected president in spite of a strong challenge from a candidate named Vuk Drašković (b. 1946) from the anticommunist and nationalist party, Serbian Renewal Movement (SRM). In addition, 194 of the Serbian assembly's 250 seats went to candidates from Milošević's new party, the Socialist Party of Serbia (SPS), a combination of the LCS and the smaller Serbian Social Alliance of Working People. The voters of Montenegro, as might be expected, showed support to their friends in the Republic of Serbia and the concept of a strong Yugoslav federation by reelecting the League of Communists to power.

At the same time, there was a strong anti-Milošević movement in Serbia, led by opposition leader Drašković. This group was in the minority but made itself highly visible by open protests against Serb leadership. In March 1991 two people were killed and hundreds injured when Serb forces broke up an anti-Milošević demonstration.

It was clear to outside observers that the once-great nation of Yugoslavia was crumbling from within. Slovenia and Croatia were the first republics to secede from the nation, in late June 1991. In response, Serb-dominated federal Yugoslav forces struck back, bombing the Slovenian airport in the republic's capital of Ljubljana. But there are very few ethnic Serbs in Slovenia, so its status meant little to Serbia.

Croatia, with its sizable ethnic Serb minority, was a different matter, and Serbia was not about to let Croatia go quietly or peacefully. The federal Yugoslav People's Army (JNA) joined forces with Serbian troops to bring the Serb sections of Croatia under their control, and by the fall they occupied a full third of Croatia. The JNA embarked on a two-pronged attack by invading Croatia from the east and at the same time conquering Croatia's historic and beautiful seaport city Dubrovnik, at the other end of the country, on the Adriatic Sea.

In September the United Nations (UN) ordered an embargo on arms shipments to Yugoslavia in an effort to stem the civil war. Cease-fires were repeatedly called, but since illegal arms were easily available, the fighting continued unabated.

That same month, voters in the Republic of Macedonia voted to establish their republic as an independent nation. In October 1991 the Republic of Bosnia and Herzegovina declared its sovereignty. Seeing the proverbial writing on the wall, sitting Yugoslav president Stipe Mesić, a Croatian, resigned his federal post and simply declared that the former nation of Yugoslavia no longer existed. In actuality, a rump Yugoslavia did exist, consisting only of the Republics of Serbia and Montenegro.

A lasting cease-fire was finally negotiated in December, and in February 1992 the United Nations sent a total of 14,000 troops to Croatia, of what was called the United Nations Protection Force (UNPROFOR). UNPROFOR moved into four Protected Areas created by the United Nations. The JNA withdrew from these areas as part of the cease-fire agreement.

In a March 1992 vote, the citizens of Montenegro decided to remain in rump Yugoslavia with Serbia, but also in March the voters of Bosnia and Herzegovina officially declared the nation's independence from Yugoslavia. To the Serbs, that was the equivalent of a red flag waved in front of a bull, and ethnic Serbs in the breakaway republic announced that they were separating themselves from the majority Muslims and forming their own Serbian Republic of Bosnia and Herzegovina.

Bosnian Serbs organized themselves into a group of terrorist cells called the Serbian Volunteer Guard. At home Vuk Drašković and other opponents of the Milošević government publicly showed that they had no patience for Serbia's aggressive acts. They held antiwar protests in the streets of Belgrade, and in one late June 1992 demonstration, roughly 100,000 people arrived to demonstrate their displeasure with the government. Drašković's new political group, the Democratic Movement of Serbia (Demos), tried to legitimately oust the ruling party by calling for a vote of "no confidence" in June, but Milošević survived.

Another election was held in the spring of 1992, this time in Kosovo. But these were illegal elections, at least according to the federal government. With Kosovo no longer holding autonomous status, the election was not recognized by the Serb-dominated government. The voters, mostly ethnic Albanians, went to the polls anyway and elected a moderate named Ibrahim Rugova (b. 1944) as their president. Rugova strongly supported the use of nonviolence to bring about social change, in the spirit of Mohandas Gandhi and Martin Luther King, Jr. The voters in Kosovo also filled the seats of the 130-member assembly, and most were won by members of the Democratic Alliance of Kosovo (DAK). Rugova and the assembly operated as a kind of "shadow government" in Kosovo.

Deeper into War

The Bosnian Serb militia under General Ratko Mladić had little trouble contending with the Muslim-dominated military of Bosnia and Herzegovina, and by summer controlled about half of the nation, including the capital, Sarajevo. Mladić's militia wrecked Bosnia's highways and commandeered Sarajevo's airport, and in 1992 a siege of Sarajevo had begun. It would last three years.

In the summer of 1992, the citizens of the world became familiar with a new term describing a new type of warfare: *ethnic cleansing*. Its purpose was to "clean out" people of an ethnic background other than one's own, and when Bosnian Serb concentration camps were discovered in Bosnia and Herzegovina, it became clear that ethnic cleansing was actively taking place.

In this case, the perpetrators were the Serbs, and the victims were Muslims and Croats who resided in places the Serbs believed should be part of a Greater Serbia. Bosnian Muslims were either forcibly removed from their homes and sent to concentration camps or killed outright. Torture was commonplace, and Muslim women were viciously raped in full view of onlookers. It was hoped that Muslim, Croats, and anyone else in the Serbs' way would fear for their life and leave their land, allowing the Serbs to move in.

However, the Serbs had no monopoly on such cruelty, which was discovered to be evident on all sides. While the Bosnian Muslims and Bosnian Croats once fought alongside each other, that alliance ended when a group of ethnic Croats living in Bosnia and Herzegovina—and fully supported by Croatia's president Franjo Tudjman—tried to fulfill dreams of a Greater Croatia in Bosnia and Herzegovina. Indeed, it later became known that Tudjman and Milošević, sworn enemies in public, had met in 1991 with the intention of working together to erase Bosnia and Herzegovina out of existence and partition it between their two countries. By the spring of 1993, the Croats of Bosnia and the Bosnian government were locked in a bitter struggle.

After the discovery of the Bosnian Serb–operated concentration camps, Yugoslavia's prime minister, Milan Panić, publicly condemned the policy of ethnic cleansing at a conference in London, England, in August 1992. However, on December 20, 1992, he ran for president of the Serb republic and lost to Milošević in an election shrouded in controversy. Opposition party leader Vuk Drašković accused Milošević of electoral improprieties. To protest what he considered a fraudulent vote, Drašković's Demos alliance, which won 49 seats in the Serbian assembly, a small minority of the total, began a boycott of Serbia's legislative body in February 1993.

The citizens of Montenegro voted similarly. No candidate won a majority of votes in the December 20, 1992, election. But in a second round of voting held on January 10, 1993, Montenegro's president, Momir Bulatović, was reelected. Bulatović's party, the Democratic Party of Montenegrin Socialists (DPMS), was formerly the League of Communists of Montenegro. So while the former Yugoslav republics favored nationalist parties, the heads of Serbia and Montenegro continued as two political peas in the pod.

As 1993 wore on and passed into 1994, Milošević used his political strength and savvy to consolidate his power in Serbia. Little could be accomplished without his approval. Across the border, in Bosnia and Herzegovina, the civil war continued. On February 5, 1994, a total of 68 civilians shopping at an outdoor market in Sarajevo were killed and more than 200 were injured by a Serb mortar shell. By 1994 television viewers throughout the world had seen news reports showing the suffering of Muslim war prisoners in Serb-run prison camps in Bosnia and Herzegovina. The international community was clamoring for a peaceful end to the carnage.

In March 1994 an agreement brokered by the United States between Bosnia and Herzegovina and Croatia resulted in a Bosniak-Croat federation. The Serbs had no part in it, though, and continued fighting. Then, former United States president Jimmy Carter helped negotiate a truce between Bosnia's Serbs and the Bosnian government. It took effect on New Year's Day, 1995, and lasted just over four months. On April 8, 1995, Bosnian Serbs attacked airplanes carrying aid to Bosniak war refugees. On May 26, the Serbs bombed Sarajevo.

After four terrible years, the war seemed to be getting only worse. Member nations of the North Atlantic Treaty Organization (NATO) came to the region to supplement militarily the UNPROFOR troops that had been sent to Bosnia in spring of 1993 to protect six "safe areas," places where refugees would not be at risk from attack.

To try and put a halt to the Serb attacks, NATO forces bombed Serb positions. Bosnian Serbs retaliated by kidnapping and holding more than 350 United Nations peacekeepers hostage, who were eventually released through negotiations. But the worst was yet to come, and it would take place in a Bosnian city called Srebrenica, about 10 miles from the border with Serbia.

Srebrenica had been designated one of the six safe areas. But under the supervision of Bosnian Serb commander Ratko Mladić, in July 1995, the Serbs turned the town into a killing field, massacring as many as 7,000 Bosnian Muslim civilians.

Then, on August 4, 1995, the action turned to Croatia, when in a surprise attack Croatian troops regained control of Krajina, a UN Protected Area in the territory held by the Serbs since 1991. The immediate result was a sea of about 160,000 Serb refugees trying to gain asylum and safety in what remained of Yugoslavia. Some were settled in Vojvodina, which angered the ethnic Hungarians living there. Even more Serb refugees were sent to Kosovo, even though the resident ethnic Albanians expressed their outrage.

After a shelling attack on a Sarajevo market on August 28th by Bosnian Serbs in which 37 people were killed and 85 injured, NATO and UNPRO-FOR troops retaliated by attacking Serb positions in Bosnia. Finally, the Serbs agreed to move their weapons from Sarajevo in mid-September, and NATO and UNPROFOR ended their retaliatory bombings.

With all sides weary of war, peace negotiations began on November 1, 1995, at Wright-Patterson Air Force Base in Dayton, Ohio. The principal parties were the United States' mediator Richard Holbrooke, Bosnia's president Alija Izetbegović, Croatia's president Franjo Tudjman, and Serbia's Slobodan Milošević. After three weeks of negotiations, a peace treaty was signed in Dayton on November 21, 1995. The war was finally over, but with an unbelievably inhumane cost: 200,000 people killed, and more than 2 million forced from their homes.

After the War

Much of the world was pessimistic about the Dayton peace agreement. A treaty is merely a written document, and the deeply held animosities among the South Slavs were so long-standing that many of the world's citizens felt the terms of the treaty would be worth little more than the paper they were printed on. War, the critics feared, would break out as soon as the ink was dry, and this time it would involve European and American NATO troops. Casualties, they speculated, would be enormous.

To the surprise of many, that did not happen—at least not as thoroughly as once thought likely. There have been periodic ethnic skirmishes, but under the supervision of the UN and NATO peacekeepers Bosnia and Herzegovina, Croatia, and Serbia and Montenegro have been at peace—albeit an uneasy peace—with one another. Problems such as the return of refugees to their homes continue to linger, but the majority of the fighting in the region is finished. However, there was one big exception: the longtime autonomous Serbian district of Kosovo.

The Kosovo War

Included in the Dayton peace agreement was a provision to find a solution to the problems in Kosovo, but no specific suggestions for accomplishing this were mentioned. Ethnic Albanians in Kosovo were especially upset that there were no demands for Serbia to restore some kind of autonomy to Kosovo. With the war in Croatia and Bosnia and Herzegovina over, the international media would focus more and more on this little district.

Politics in Belgrade in the immediate years after the war were anything but placid. Anti-Milošević forces continued to protest the Serb president's ironfisted way of governing, but by the spring of 1997 the strongest organized opposition had fizzled, leaving Milošević in uncontested leadership. In mid-July 1997, during a special parliamentary session, the Yugoslav federal assembly elected Milošević as president of Yugoslavia. Members of the opposition boycotted the vote, but to no avail. On July 23, 1997, Milošević officially stepped down as president of Serbia and was inaugurated as president of the entire country.

A general election was slated for Montenegro on October 7, 1997; no candidate cleared a majority, so a second election took place on October 19. A young reformist, Milo Djukanović (b. 1962) narrowly defeated incumbent Momir Bulatović (b. 1956) of the Democratic Party of Montenegrin Socialists (DPMS), an ally of Milošević. Bulatović's supporters immediately claimed that Djukanovič and his staff commandeered the election by using fake voting lists, but the Organization for Security and Cooperation in Europe (OSCE), an alliance of European nations that observed the elections, said nothing illegal had taken place. What made the election of Djukanović noteworthy is that this Montenegrin leader, unlike most in the past, parted political company with Serbia. Djukanović publicly criticized Milošević, claiming in a published interview that he was unfit to hold office.

In mid-January Djukanović was sworn in as president of Montenegro, while violent protests went on in the streets of Montenegro's capital city of Podgorica. After two members of Montenegro's police force were killed in the unrest, the government of Montenegro banned such public protests. In May 1998 Milošević repaid Bulatović for his loyalty by nominating him to the office of federal prime minister, a move approved by

Milo Djukanović was elected president of Montenegro on January 15, 1998. (Photo copyright Pedja Milosavljević)

the Yugoslav assembly. The new post for Bulatović was denounced by the Montenegrin government, and for a while the Montenegrins seriously considered declaring their independence from Yugoslavia.

Most of the eyes of the world were not on Montenegro, with its political tension, but on Kosovo, where war was brewing. Kosovan president Ibrahim Rugova continued his nonviolent tactics, such as boycotting the federal government. But a group of Kosovo citizens was frustrated with Rugova's methods and formed a small guerilla force called the Kosovo Liberation Army (KLA). The KLA soon started its own battle with Serb authorities in Kosovo.

On February 28, 1998, Serbian officials began a campaign to destroy the KLA and ongoing fighting between Serb police and the KLA became standard. (Although Montenegro was part of Yugoslavia, the republic did not take an active part in the conflict in Kosovo.) A particularly vicious attack took place in a region of Kosovo called Drenica, west of the Kosovan capital of Priština. While the intended purpose of the assault may have been a crackdown on the operations of the KLA, it was clear that ethnic Albanian civilians were the majority of victims. Accounts varied, but most said that more than 100 people in the villages of Izbica, Prekaz, and Luasha were killed.

SLOBODAN MILOŠEVIĆ

Born on August 29, 1941, in the small Serbian town of Požarevac, a bit southeast of Belgrade, Milošević was the product of a broken home and an unhappy childhood. His father, a schoolteacher named Svetozar, walked out on his family some time around 1946. In 1962 his father committed suicide by shooting himself in the head.

Slobodan was raised almost entirely by his mother, Stanislava, also a teacher and a very partisan communist. She too committed suicide, 10 years after her husband, by hanging herself in the family living room. One of Milošević's uncles, an army general, also committed suicide, raising questions about the mental health in his family.

In high school, Milošević met his future wife, Mirjana Marcović, a devout communist from a well-known Serbian communist family. They would have two children, a son, Marko, and a daughter, Marija.

Milošević joined Tito's League of Communists of Yugoslavia (LCY) in 1959 and became an expert in economics and business. He served as economics adviser to the mayor of Belgrade; director general of the state-owned gas company, Technogas; and then president of the United Bank of Belgrade. In 1983 and 1984, he was a member of the LCY's central committee, and from 1984 to 1986 he headed Belgrade's Communist Party organization.

Milošević's wife, Mirjana, known familiarly as Mira, became a professor of sociology at the University of Belgrade, and as Slobodan worked his way up the hierarchy of the Communist government, she also became his political partner. Mira boldly predicted that her husband would be a renowned Communist leader as great as Marshal Tito.

Her prediction was partly true. He did become as famous as Tito, but for considerably more infamous actions. And while many political correspondents have portrayed him as a true villain, some of the same analysts praised him in 1995 for the part he took in making the 1995 Dayton peace agreement possible. He is a truly complex figure, and it is likely that analysts will be examining his life for generations to come.

One resident of Izbica reported, "The Serbs came, began shouting, threw us out of our homes and took everything we had. Then they separated the men from the women and children and chased them out of the village. The men were kept back. We were put in three different lines. They began shooting."

Watchdog organizations were outraged. Daan Everts, a representative of the OSCE said, "We cannot let the perpetrators of such hideous crimes go unpunished. This should trigger even more intensive efforts to put an end to this conflict."

The United States, as it had four years earlier, kept a close eye on the situation. Secretary of State Madeleine Albright warned, "We must not allow President Milošević's brutal and illegitimate methods there to undo the progress toward peace and stability that has been made throughout the region." The United States and European powers, including France, Great Britain, Italy, Germany, and even Serbia's traditional ally, Russia, agreed, in the words of Albright, "to deny President Milošević resources for his police state."

By the summer, the violence had escalated into an all-out civil war, and as Everts advised, the OSCE and NATO took action. A cease-fire negotiated by diplomats from NATO was declared on October 25, 1998. Groups of OSCE peace monitors were sent to Kosovo. But the cease-fire did not last even two months. In December the KLA and Yugoslav forces began fighting once more, and on January 15, 1999, the Yugoslav military killed 45 ethnic Albanians in an attack in the village of Racak.

NATO representatives tried again to bring the violence to an end. Representatives of the KLA and Yugoslavia met to talk peace in a castle in Rambouillet, outside Paris, France in February 1999. The primary goals were for Yugoslav forces to withdraw from Kosovo and for Kosovo to return to its status as an autonomous region inside Yugoslavia, but administered by NATO peacekeeping troops. Representatives of the KLA and other ethnic Albanian participants signed a treaty, but Yugoslavia did not, claiming it supported autonomy but did not trust NATO, preferring the United Nations to oversee peacekeeping efforts.

However, some political analysts believe that the KLA never had its heart in the agreement and signed only because they knew it would never be approved by Yugoslavia. These observers argue that the KLA wanted only full independence from Yugoslavia. Without approval from the Milošević government, the Rambouillet accords fell apart.

With the peace talks in ruins, Milošević sent his military into action, and Serb-led assaults on ethnic Albanians grew more frequent and more ruthless. NATO forces, having tried and failed at peace negotiations, responded to Serbia's actions on March 24 by launching air strikes against

THE KOSOVO LIBERATION ARMY

The KLA began around 1996 with just a few dozen members and mainly resorted to ambush killings of Serb law enforcement figures. But it grew quickly, mainly because of support from the nation of Albania in the forms of money and military equipment. By the end of 1998, the KLA had become a legitimate force in the Kosovo civil war. Estimates gave it anywhere from 5,000 to 12,000 members at its peak.

A total figure is hard to come by, though, since the KLA was not a unified military group under the authority of a government. It was organized mostly in small cells, and its members represented a wide range of political goals. Some members supported Islamic nationalism, some were procommunist, and some saw themselves as homegrown soldiers with varied intentions, from freeing Kosovo of Serb authority to its own ethnic cleansing of Serbs.

A member of the New York–based group Human Rights Watch, Fred Abrahams, said of the KLA in 1998, "When you encounter them, you may meet a villager with a hunting rifle defending his home, or someone who clearly has had military training—and everything in between."

At first, the KLA operated by firing on Serbian police in Kosovo, which the KLA hoped would lead the police officers into wooden areas, where they would be ambushed and killed. Although most of the first KLA victims were not high-ranking police officials, after the massacre at Drenica, the KLA broadened their actions, attacking more important

Serbian military targets. Throughout the months of April and May, the hell of war fell over Kosovo. Serbian forces led assaults on ethnic Albanians, burning their villages and creating hundreds of thousands of refugees; these people then risked personal attacks, such as robberies by Serbs, to find safe havens across the border in countries, such as Albania and Macedonia, or in Montenegro. Concerned that Milošević was reckless and power hungry and might next try to overtake their republic, the leaders of Montenegro cooperated with NATO.

In response to the Serbian aggression, NATO bombers stepped up their attacks on strategic Serbian targets, such as oil production facilities, bridges, and highways, including those in the capital city of Belgrade. However, the NATO forces, who considered themselves the good guys

Serbian police units and facilities. It then further expanded its range of attacks, targeting Serb armed forces and roadways with the intention of interrupting supply transportation. Whether the KLA is seen as a terrorist organization or a group of freedom fighters depends on which side the observer is on.

An ethnic Albanian militant scouts out Serb police positions in southern Serbia's Preševo Valley near the Kosovo border in December 2000.
(AP Photo/Visar Kryeziu)

trying to stop more ethnic cleansing as they had four years earlier, were getting their own share of criticism. Critics said NATO's air strikes were aggravating the situation by making Serbia even more determined to fight back. Reports came out that their "humanitarian bombardment" was negligent and inadvertently killed many ethnic Albanians—the very same people they were trying to save. Milošević exploited these criticisms, using the international media to accuse the NATO bombings, not the Serb attacks, of causing the huge refugee problem.

On April 12, a NATO airplane dropped a bomb on a railroad bridge in southern Serbia, with the intent of crippling the Serbian transportation system. But the bomb hit a passenger train that was crossing the bridge, and about 12 civilians on the train were killed. Then, on

May 7, NATO bombs mistakenly fell on the Chinese embassy in Belgrade. Not only were three embassy workers killed and nearly two dozen injured, but it caused a diplomatic nightmare. NATO representatives apologized and said the bombing error was caused by an outdated map they had been given by the Central Intelligence Agency (CIA) of the United States. The Chinese government did not care, and it reacted with anger, straining relations between China and the NATO countries.

Discussions among the NATO nations about sending in ground troops then took place. Perhaps this might help expedite a conclusion to the war and lessen the chance of more bombing errors, they thought. In late May, NATO went ahead and approved moving 50,000 peacekeeping troops to territory near Kosovo's borders.

A legal matter helped bring a quick end to the civil war. Back in 1993, the United Nations, having discovered the truth of the rumors of ethnic cleansing, passed a resolution establishing the International Criminal Tribunal for the Former Yugoslavia (ICTY), the first international body for the prosecution of war crimes since the end of World War II. Based in The Hague, in the Netherlands, the tribunal has jurisdiction for persons accused of war crimes, crimes against humanity, and genocide in former Yugoslavia since January 1, 1991. On May 27, 1999, the U.N. War Crimes Tribunal issued a warrant for the arrest of Milošević and four other Serb leaders for war crimes, including genocide, crimes against humanity, grave breaches of the Geneva conventions, and violations of the laws or customs of war.

On the battlefield, the Serbs were being beaten by the KLA, whose numbers now were estimated at around 20,000. Because of the NATO air campaigns, Serb soldiers were forced to entrench themselves in positions in which they were open to KLA attacks. Meanwhile, the Serbs' close allies, the Russians, were trying to convince Milošević to accept a peace plan on behalf of NATO. Aware of the Serbs' and his own vulnerability, Milošević, on June 3, agreed to an international peace plan.

Among the principles of the agreement were the following:

- an "immediate and verifiable end to the violence and repression in Kosovo"

- "withdrawal from Kosovo of military, police and paramilitary forces"
- the "establishment of an interim administration for Kosovo to be decided by the Security Council of the United Nations to ensure conditions for a peaceful and normal life for all inhabitants in Kosovo"
- "the safe and free return of all refugees and displaced persons and unimpeded access to Kosovo by humanitarian aid organizations"
- "a political process towards the establishment of an interim political framework agreement providing for a substantial self-government for Kosovo, taking full account of the Rambouillet accords and the principles of sovereignty and territorial integrity of the Federal Republic of Yugoslavia and the other countries of the region, and the demilitarization of the KLA"
- the "comprehensive approach to the economic development and stabilization of the crisis region."

On June 10, NATO forces stopped their bombing campaign. It had lasted 78 days. With the war over, roughly 850,000 Kosovan refugees began returning home, and about 200,000 Serb civilians and their supporters, fearing revenge attacks by ethnic Albanians, left Kosovo for Serbia proper. In the days immediately following the war, Kosovo was handed over to a U.N. administration and a NATO-led peacekeeping force, then divided into five military sections patrolled by American, British, French, German, and Italian troops. It would cost billions of dollars to first feed and house the war's victims, then to rebuild the infrastructure of the war-ravaged region.

The Aftermath

In the months following the war, Slobodan Milošević became more and more withdrawn, making few public appearances, eventually to the point that his own advisers did not see him for weeks at a time. Montenegro, for so long a loyal supporter of Serbia, was distancing itself more and more from the Serb republic in general and Milošević in particular. The Yugoslav leader seemed to be alienated from the same average Serb citizens for whom he had spoken for so many years. Then, in a general election that took place on October 7, 2000, opposition leader Vojislav Koštunica (b. 1944) was elected president of Yugoslavia.

Milošević did not leave without a fight. While he admitted that Koštunica received more votes than he, Milošević refused to accept the election results as final, saying they were so close that a special runoff election was needed. In response, Koštunica supporters, organized by both Koštunica and Serb opposition leader Zoran Djindjić (1952–2003) rioted in the streets of Belgrade against Milošević, who called out the federal military to forcefully end the uprising. However, the military turned against Milošević and refused to follow his orders. Milošević had no choice but to step down, and Koštunica took office as the new president of the Federal Republic of Yugoslavia.

Djindjić emphasized the earnestness of the situation when he told an interviewer, "Milošević made it clear that it was either him or me. We had to beat him otherwise he would have arrested us and killed us at the first opportunity. That made it easy for us. We knew we had to win."

In January 2001 Zoran Djindjić was elected the first noncommunist prime minister of Serbia in modern times, receiving a hearty 64 percent of the vote. Democratic elections were slated for much of Yugoslavia in 2001. Parties in favor of Montenegrin independence won majorities, and Filip Vujanović (b. 1954) was reelected in that republic's elections on April 22, 2001. Ibrahim Rugova became president of Kosovo as his moderate Democratic League of Kosovo won a plurality in his province's general elections on November 19, 2001.

One of the most momentous days in the region's history was March 14, 2002: It was announced then that Yugoslavia, a country in some form since the conclusion of World War I, had officially come to an end as a nation. Serbia and Montenegro signed an agreement restructuring what was left of the federation, giving each republic greater autonomy and the nation a new official name: Serbia and Montenegro. Vojislav Koštunica, who remained president of the nation until his post was dissolved, said at the time, "This document sets the shape of completely new relations between the states of Serbia and Montenegro. This step means a break with the previous regime," referring to Milošević. "Amid the threat of disintegration in the Balkans, we are moving towards integration and peace and stability in the region." The new name and the new nation were officially adopted on February 4, 2003.

But, on March 12, 2003, history proved that despite signs of progress, some things remain the same in the region. Serbia's reformist prime minister Zoran Djindjić was assassinated by a band of snipers in Belgrade. Members of a paramilitary group called the Red Berets, allegedly connected to organized crime, have been charged with the murder. It is believed they wanted to install a government made up of allies of Milošević.

However, controversy ensued during the criminal investigation into the assassination. Almost 2,000 people were arrested during the murder probe, called Operation Saber. On September 4, 2003, human rights watchdog group Amnesty International released a report accusing the federal government of torturing suspects and other detainees.

The report stated, "We believe that the use of torture and ill treatment during Operation Saber was widespread, particularly against those perceived as being relatively low-level criminals, out of the public eye and unlikely to have their allegations widely publicized. . . . These are extremely serious allegations, and we are asking the Serbian authorities

Funeral procession for assassinated leader Zoran Djindjić on April 20, 2003.
(Photo copyright Pedja Milosavljević)

to allow us and other human rights groups unfettered access to interview any of the detainees privately, so that we may ascertain the true scale of the problem."

Federal authorities have repeatedly denied allegations of torture.

NOTES

p. 43 "The unemployment level . . ." Misha Glenny, *The Balkans: Nationalism, War and the Great Powers, 1804–1999.* New York: Viking Penguin, 2000, p. 623.

p. 43 "In 1982 the debt . . ." Ibid.

p. 46 "Milošević called out words . . ." Robert Thomas, *The Politics of Serbia in the 1990s.* New York: Columbia University Press, 1999, p. 44.

p. 46 "But in 1989 . . ." Robert J. Donia and John V. A. Fine, Jr., *Bosnia and Herzegovina: A Tradition Betrayed.* New York: Columbia University Press, 1994, p. 199.

p. 48 "In addition, 194 of the Serbian assembly's . . ." "Yugoslavia," *Europa World Book.* New York: Europa Publications, 2002, p. 4438.

p. 49 "A lasting cease-fire . . ." Ibid. p. 4439

p. 52 "But under the supervision . . ." "World Europe Srebrenica report blames UN." BBC. (November 16, 1999) Available on-line. URL:http://news.bbc.co.uk/1/hi/world/europe/521825.stm. Downloaded September 13, 2002.

p. 53 "The war was finally over . . ." "Bosnian leaders embrace new era." (July 15, 2002) Available on-line. URL: http://news.bbc.co.uk/2/hi/europe/2128641.stm. Downloaded September 14, 2002.

p. 56 "One resident of Izbica reported . . ." Amanda Kibel, "Survivors describe the death of a village," CNN. (May 19, 1999) Available on-line. URL: http://www.cnn.com/WORLD/europe/9905/19/massacre.index.html. Downloaded May 9, 2003.

p. 57 "Daan Everts, a representative of . . ." Ibid.

p. 57 "Secretary of State Madeleine Albright . . ." Jane A. Morse, "US Prepared to take additional steps in Kosovo, Albright says," USIS Washington file. Available on-line. URL: http://usembassy-australia.state.gov/hyper/WF980318/epf302.htm. Downloaded May 8, 2003.

p. 57 "The United States and European powers . . ." Ibid.

p. 58 "A member of the New York–based group . . ." "Surging Insurgency," Online NewsHour. (July 15, 1998) Available on-line. URL: http://www.pbs.org/newshour/bb/europe/july-dec98/kla_7-15.html. Downloaded May 10, 2003.

pp. 60–61 "Among the principles . . ." "Resolution 1244 (1999) Adopted by the Security Council at its 4011th meeting, on 10 June 1999," NATO. Available on-line. URL: http://www.nato.int/kosovo/docu/u990610a.htm. Downloaded May 9, 2003.

p. 61 "With the war over . . ." Tim Judah, " Milošević: Serbia's fallen strongman." (March 30, 2001) Available on-line. URL: http://news.bbc.co.uk/1/hi/world/europe/931018.stm. Downloaded May 10, 2003.

p. 62 "Djindjić emphasized the earnestness . . ." "Obituary: Zoran Djindjić" (March 13, 2003) Available on-line. URL: http://news.bbc.co.uk/go/pr/fr/-/hi/world/europe/2844081.stm. Downloaded May 10, 2003.

p. 62 "In January 2001 Zoran Djindjič . . ." Ibid.

p. 62 "'This document sets the shape . . .'" "Yugoslavia no more: Meet 'Serbia and Montenegro,'" Associated Press. (March 14, 2002) Available on-line. URL: http://www.usatoday.com/news/world/2002/03/14/yugoslavia-no-more.htm. Downloaded January 9, 2003.

pp. 63–64 "'We believe that . . .'" "Rights Group Urges Inquiry on Torture in Serbia," *New York Times*, September 4, 2003.

PART II
Serbia and Montenegro Today

4

GOVERNMENT

Serbia and Montenegro may be old lands, but they have an almost brand new government. As Yugoslavia, the two republics had adopted a constitution on April 27, 1992, which called for a federal president, a prime minister, a deputy prime minister, and eight federal ministers—foreign affairs, finance, justice, defense, internal affairs, the economy and domestic trade, transportation and telecommunications, and national and ethnic groups—equivalent to the secretaries of different cabinet departments in the United States. In addition, both Serbia and Montenegro had their own presidents, prime ministers, deputy prime ministers, and ministers of numerous departments.

The Yugoslav federal assembly, or *savezna skupština*, was composed of two bodies: The Chamber of Citizens was comprised of 138 persons (108 from Serbia and 30 from Montenegro) directly elected for four-year terms. The other unit, the Chamber of Republics, consisted of 40 members (20 each from Serbia and Montenegro). Finally, there was a judicial branch of the former nation. Its most powerful organ was the Federal Court, consisting of 11 judges elected by the *savezna skupština*.

A New Nation and a New Constitution

When Yugoslavia's leaders agreed to the reorganization of their country and the establishment of the new nation of Serbia and Montenegro on March 14, 2002, it was noted that the federal, Serbian, and Montenegrin

4

4

assemblies needed to undertake the drafting of a new constitutional charter. A provisional agreement of principles was drawn up, with the intent that it might be used as the basis of a permanent constitution. Once a proposed constitutional text was adopted, it would have to be approved by the two republic assemblies, and then by the federal assembly.

Some provisions of the new government were agreed upon at that time. One was a basic acceptance that the newly reorganized union was an experiment. It was declared that after a period of three years both Serbia and Montenegro would be eligible to try to change their statehood status or even to secede from the new union. Since it was unlikely that more populous and more powerful Serbia would want to leave the union, that provision applied mainly to Montenegro. It was declared that if Montenegro was to secede, any international agreements made by Serbia and Montenegro with any other country would relate in their entirety to Serbia as the nation's successor. However, if both republics opted for independence, issues such as agreements with other nations would be resolved in the succession procedure, as was done with the former Federal Republic of Yugoslavia.

Over the next several months, there was bickering, pressure from other European countries, and finally conciliatory agreements among the citizens and leaders of Serbia and Montenegro. In May 2002 the federal government took a first step toward a permanent change when it ratified an accord ending the Yugoslav federation, thereby clearing a path for the drawing up of a new constitution for Serbia and Montenegro. A constitution was devised over the course of the summer, and on November 29, 2002, the three leaders—Yugoslav federation head Vojislav Koštunica, Serbian prime minister Zoran Djindjić, and Montenegrin leader Milo Djukanović—agreed to accept the new nation's constitutional charter. The next month, the two republics' parliaments accepted it. A cochairman of the committee drafting the constitution, Dragan Jocić, announced, "We can freely say we are beginning to build a new house where there will be room for both families."

But there was one more step to go for final approval. That took place on February 4, 2003, when the federal parliament approved the constitutional charter and, in doing so, sent the nation of Yugoslavia into the annals of history.

The Constitution

The basics of the new constitution are outlined in its first three articles. It is clear that the founders of the newly reorganized nation are making a special effort to be certain that the horrors of the 1990s are never repeated. This is duly noted in Article 3, listed below.

THE NAME
Article 1
The name of the State union shall be Serbia and Montenegro.

PRINCIPLE OF EQUALITY
Article 2
Serbia and Montenegro shall be based on the equality of the two member states, the state of Serbia and the state of Montenegro.

GOALS
Article 3
The goals of Serbia and Montenegro shall be:

respect for the human rights of all persons within its competence,

preservation and promotion of human dignity, equality and the rule of law,

integration in European structures, the European Union in particular,

harmonization of its legislation and practices with European and international standards

introduction of market economy based on free enterprise, competition and social justice, and

establishment and ensurance [sic] of an unhindered operation of the common market on its territory through coordination and harmonization of the economic systems of the member states in line with the principle and standards of the European Union.

More important declarations, especially in light of Serbia's recent history, are spelled out in Article 9:

EXERCISE OF HUMAN AND
MINORITY RIGHTS AND CIVIL LIBERTIES
Article 9

The member states shall regulate, ensure and protect human and minority rights and civil liberties on their territories.

The achieved level of human and minority rights, individual and collective, and of civil liberties may not be reduced.

Serbia and Montenegro shall monitor the implementation of human and minority rights and civil liberties and shall ensure their protection if such protection is not ensured in the member states.

SVETOZVAR MAROVIĆ

The first president of the new nation of Serbia and Montenegro has a challenge ahead of him that will indeed require true determination to overcome.

After being sworn into office on March 7, 2003, Marović announced that his "ultimate goal at all levels is the Europeanization of Montenegro and Serbia." He called for mutual confidence and understanding between the two republics, warning, "Neither Serbia, nor Montenegro can hope to proceed more speedily through these processes if one does something to the detriment of the other. . . . By adopting European rules of living and political activities, we will make the best contribution to resolving problems in the region, such as the problem of Kosovo, which must be resolved strictly through dialogue and with the help of the international community."

Marović expressed confidence that "the time of sabre-rattling, ethnic conflicts and wars in the Balkans is definitely over."

The man who spoke those words of reassurance and confidence was born on March 31, 1955, in the historic medieval town of Kotor on Montenegro's coast. He graduated from the Montenegrin capital city of Podgorica's law school before settling in another historic coastal town, Budva.

Marović is cofounder and deputy chairman of the Montenegrin Democratic Party of Socialists (DPS), which in its early days advocated independence. He was elected a member of Montenegro's parliament in 1990 and was a noted member of the Montenegrin government, serving as its speaker three times between 1994 and 2001, until becoming president of the Montenegrin parliament. Marović gained

According to the nation's new constitution, Serbia and Montenegro's federal government consists of three branches: executive, legislative, and judicial. The federal government's main role is to provide a military, conduct foreign affairs, and supervise human rights activities. The head of state is the president, a post filled by Svetozvar Marović (b. 1955) in March 2003. Under the president are the prime minister, described as the head of government, as opposed to the head of state, and a deputy prime minister.

The president serves a four-year term and is elected not directly by the people but by parliament. The speaker and deputy speaker of parliament

experience in dealing with other countries by heading the Montenegrin parliament's foreign affairs commission.

Marović was elected president of Serbia and Montenegro by receiving 65 votes of the 112 votes (one vote per member) members of parliament; his opponents received 47 (14 members were absent).

In addition to his duties as a statesman, Marović is an avid writer, having authored numerous articles for newspapers and magazines, and is also a major cultural booster, initiating a variety of cultural events for the city of Budva. He is married and the father of two children.

From left, Serbia and Montenegro president Svetozvar Marović, Montenegrin prime minister Milo Djukanović and his wife Lidija, and newly elected Montenegrin president Filip Vujanović gather at Vujanović's inauguration ceremony in Cetinje on June 13, 2003. (AP Photo/Risto Bozović)

propose a presidential candidate to the parliament. If the candidate does not received a majority of the votes required, the speaker and deputy speaker have 10 days to select a new candidate. If this second candidate fails to receive a majority of votes, the parliament is dissolved, and new general elections are held.

In order to maintain fair representation for both republics, the constitution mandates that should the elected president come from the same republic as the speaker of parliament, then the speaker and deputy speaker will switch their roles. Also, the president shall not come from the same member state twice in succession.

Parliament, Parties, and Judges

Unlike the former Yugoslav legislature, the new parliament of Serbia and Montenegro consists of just one body. It has 126 seats total; 91 representatives come from Serbia and 35 from Montenegro. For the 2003–05 term of office, the first session following the adoption of the charter, the parliament was filled by nominees from the individual parliaments of the Republics of Serbia and Montenegro. For each session after that, the president will call for public elections, and members of parliament will serve four-year terms of office. Any resident age 18 or older may vote in a federal election; employed persons as young as 16 can also vote.

Like its Balkan counterparts, Serbia and Montenegro boasts a large number—at least a dozen—legitimate and recognized political parties. In 2003 the majority party in the parliament, with 37 seats, was the Democratic Opposition of Serbia (DOS), which itself is an alliance of 13 smaller parties. It was put together in the 1990s as an anti-Milošević party and comprises at least four parties originally based in Vojvodina, along with several other parties headquartered in Serbia proper.

Another new party holding a sizable number of members of parliament, 19 in 2003, is a smaller coalition of parties known as the Democratic List for European Montenegro (DLECG), consisting of the moderate to liberal Social Democratic Party of Montenegro (SDP), which has advocated independence for Montenegro; the Democratic Party of Socialists for Montenegro (DPS), led by Svetozvar Marović; and three smaller parties. Other parties with between 12 and 17 seats in parliament are the Socialist Party of Serbia (SPS), which favors Serb nationalism, and was founded by Milošević; the Democratic Party of Serbia (DSS), a moderate nationalist party that bolted from the DOS alliance in 2001; and an opposition coalition called Together for Changes (ZP). Together for Changes comprises smaller opposing parties, including the Socialist People's Party (SNP), the Serbian People's Party (SNS), and the People's Party (NS).

Serbia and Montenegro's supreme court is called the Federal Court. Its main functions, similar to those of the United States Supreme Court, are to discern the constitutionality of its nation's laws and to settle disputes between institutions in Serbia and Montenegro as they pertain to the constitution. These decisions could relate to everything from complaints by private citizens that their constitutional rights have been violated to rulings on whether the member states' own constitutions are in conformity with the federal constitution. Federal court judges are elected by the federal parliament for one six-year term; they may not be reelected. To be eligible, each candidate must have a degree in law and at least 15 years in the legal profession.

The Council of Ministers

The president's cabinet, or council of ministers, with only five members, is relatively small compared to those of other nations. Ministers are voted in by the federal parliament after being recommended by the president. They serve terms of four years. The council consists of:

1. the minister of foreign affairs, responsible for Serbia and Montenegro's foreign policy, including the negotiation of international treaties and the proposal of candidates to head the country's diplomatic and consular missions;
2. the minister of defense, who by law must be a civilian, responsible for coordinating and implementing the nation's defense policy, as well as for running its military forces;
3. the minister for international economic cooperation, responsible for negotiating the implementation of international treaties and maintaining sound relations with international banks and other financial institutions;

4. the minister for internal economic cooperation, responsible for coordinating the economic systems of both member states in order to maintain a free movement of goods, services, people, and capital; and

5. the minister for human and minority rights, responsible for monitoring such rights as they are exercised throughout the nation, in addition to ensuring the implementation and respect of international conventions on the protection of human and minority rights.

Two candidates for ministers must be from the same state as the president, with the remaining three from the other member state. Another requirement is that midway through their terms the ministers of foreign affairs and defense switch posts and take on their respective deputies and duties.

Local Government

Unlike the United States, Serbia and Montenegro's two divisions are much more independent from the federal government. Each republic maintains its own currency, and each has its own customs services. Each also has its own government.

The republics of Serbia and Montenegro have their own local governments. Serbia is led by a president, six deputy prime ministers, and a secretary general. There are 18 ministers of departments, including internal affairs, economy and privatization, energy and mining, religion, health, and education and sport. There are also 29 parliamentary committees, including health and family, agriculture, relations with Serbs outside Serbia, and sexual equality.

The Serbian assembly is a unicameral body of 250 seats filled by deputies. Each is elected for a four-year term. The assembly is led by a president, two vice presidents, and a secretary. In 2003 all the top posts with the exception of one vice president were held by women. The republic of Serbia also has an independent judiciary.

Montenegro's republican government consists of a president, prime minister, one or more deputy prime ministers, and several ministers. The president is elected for a term of five years and may serve a maximum of two terms. There is one exception to that law: If Montenegro is actively at war, the president's term is extended until peace has been established.

Like that of the Republic of Serbia, Montenegro's assembly consists of deputies elected to four-year terms. And like the terms of Montenegro's president, if Montenegro is actively at war, deputies' terms are extended for as long as the war continues. Rather than call for a definite number of deputies, the Montenegrin constitution states that one deputy shall be elected for every 6,000 voters. So if the population of Montenegro is 650,000, there will be 108 deputies in the assembly. Montenegro also has an independent judiciary.

Human Rights and the United Nations War Crimes Tribunal

When reports of ethnic cleansing were verified during the Balkan civil war of 1991–95, members of the United Nations decided to reestablish the concept of an international war crimes tribunal. At the end of World War II, an international body for the prosecution of war crimes was established to investigate the criminal acts of Germany and Japan during that war. As a result, war crimes courts were held in Nuremberg, Germany, and Tokyo, Japan.

Member nations of the United Nations felt that such a body was necessary for the war crimes of the early 1990s in Yugoslavia and Rwanda. On May 25, 1993, the United Nations Security Council passed Resolution 827 establishing the International Criminal Tribunal for the Former Yugoslavia (ICTY), to be based in The Hague, in the Netherlands. The ICTY has jurisdiction for persons accused of war crimes, crimes against humanity, and genocide in former Yugoslavia occurring since January 1, 1991. However, it cannot try suspects in absentia (without the suspect physically present in the court), nor may it impose the death penalty; the steepest sentence it can hand down is life imprisonment.

The ICTY has large teams of investigators working throughout the former Yugoslavian republics, but it does not maintain a police force. Therefore, it is dependent on police in the former Yugoslavia and international peace forces, such as UNPROFOR, to make arrests and turn over suspects. To try and assure objectivity, the United Nations has placed an international array of officers and judges in the ICTY; they represent nations as disparate as France, Zambia, Portugal, Switzerland, the United Kingdom, and Australia.

Serbia has had a less than satisfactory record in cooperating with the ICTY. When Slobodan Milošević was in office, Serbia's official stance regarding the war crimes tribunal was that it was a creation of NATO in general and the United States in particular, with the intention of persecuting Serbia for conducting what the Serbs considered a legitimate war. For a long time, Serbia's lack of cooperation extended even to refusing to provide evidence that might help Serb victims of war crimes allegedly committed by Croats or Bosnians. While awaiting trial in January 2002. Milošević claimed that he was the victim and that NATO forces, especially those involved with the NATO bombings in 1999, were the perpetrators.

Said Milošević of the tribunal's efforts to try him, "I would call this an evil and hostile attack aimed at justifying the crimes committed against my country." He added that the trial "was an attempt to turn the victim into the culprit."

After the fall of Milošević, Serb leaders began to work to some degree with the tribunal. Milošević was turned over to the ICTY in late June 2001. He faces three indictments: one for crimes in Croatia between 1991 and 1992, another for atrocities in Kosovo in 1999, and, the most serious, for genocide in Bosnia and Herzegovina between 1992 and 1995.

Even after Milošević was handed over, some members of the tribunal accused Serbia of dragging its feet in terms of finding and turning over other wanted suspects. Some Serbs complained that the ICTY was guilty of ethnic prejudice against the Serbs. They cited the fact that more than half of those publicly charged—at least 40 out of 75 indictees—are Serbs. Croats and Bosnians countered by stating that Serbs were responsible for most of the war crimes. Serbs also criticized the fact that Croatia's Franjo Tudjman was never charged with any crimes by the ICTY.

In May 2003 Serbia and Montenegro president Svetozvar Marović told the ICTY chief prosecutor Carla Del Ponte of Switzerland that Serbia would be happy to turn over wanted war crimes suspects but many were in hiding and could not be found. These included some accused of the most serious charges of genocide, such as Bosnian Serb general Ratko Mladić and Bosnian Serb wartime leader Radovan Karadžić.

The United States and other NATO nations have continued to put pressure on Serbia and Montenegro to extradite Serb war crime suspects to the tribunal. Failing to do so would put Serbia and Montenegro at risk of losing financial aid and other support. On May 17, 2003, Serb authorities did turn over to the tribunal a former JNA army officer named Miroslav Radić, wanted for supervising the Serb troops who had murdered about 200 civilians near the town of Vukovar, Croatia, in 1991.

Six Months After

About a half-year after the formal establishment of Serbia and Montenegro, many observers reported that the country was hardly gelling as one nation. Problems were reported in everything from bureaucratic tie-ups in crossing the border from one republic to the other to complaints from Serbs that Montenegro was blocking progress toward joining the European Union.

Some were predicting the worst. A Belgrade-based European Union official named Willem Blankert was one of those who voiced pessimism. He said of the union of Serbia and Montenegro in August 2003, "Yes, it is difficult. I give it less than a 50 percent chance [for success]."

Others hoped the new nation would succeed, but were cautionary. A former federal deputy prime minister, Miroljob Labus, said, "In my view, it should be one country. But, you know, there is no political determination in Montenegro for that. The reality is that we have two states with a very weak connection."

NOTES

p. 70 "A cochairman of the committee . . ." "Accord agreed on Yugoslavia's future," BBC. (December 7, 2002) Available on-line. URL: http://news.bbc.co.uk/1/hi/world/europe/2552387.stm. Downloaded May 29, 2003.

p. 71 "The basics of the new constitution . . ." "The Constitutional Charter of The State Union of Serbia and Montenegro," Serbia and Montenegro Ministry of Foreign Affairs. Available on-line. URL: http://www.mfa.gov.yu/Facts/chartere.html. Downloaded May 29, 2003.

p. 72 "'The member states shall regulate . . .'" "The Constitutional Charter of the State Union of Serbia and Montenegro."

p. 72 "After being sworn into office . . ." "Yugoslav Daily Survey," Ministry of Foreign Affairs, Yugoslavia. (March 9, 2003) Available on-line. URL: http://news.serbianunity.net/bydate/2003/march_10/0.html. Downloaded May 31, 2003.

p. 72 "'Neither Serbia, nor Montenegro . . .'" "Yugoslav Daily Survey."

p. 72 "Marović expressed confidence . . ." "Yugoslav Daily Survey."

p. 73 "Marović was elected president . . ." "Yugoslav Daily Survey."

p. 78 "Said Milošević of the tribunals' efforts . . ." Vivienne Walt. "War Crimes Trial of Milošević Begins Today," *USA Today*, February 12, 2002, p. 11A.

p. 78 "He added that the trial . . ." Walt, "War Crimes Trial of Milošević Begins Today."

p. 78 "They cited the fact that . . ." "The ICTY at a Glance," United Nations. (May 30, 2003) Available on-line. URL: http://www.un.org/icty/glance/glancetleft-e.htm. Downloaded May 31, 2003.

p. 79 "Yes, it is difficult." Ian Fisher, "Newest Balkan State in a State of Stress." *New York Times*. August 12, 2003.

p. 79 "A former federal deputy . . ." *New York Times*, August 12 2003.

5

RELIGION

Like those of other South Slav nations, the people of Serbia and Montenegro have an ambivalent attitude toward religion. The citizens of this country are generally not very devout, and religion plays a relatively small role in public life. For decades under Tito, Yugoslavia was officially an atheist nation. Yet the people's religions signify who they are; they are sources of ethnic pride more than creeds.

Serbia and Montenegro has for a long time been identified with the Orthodox Christian Church, and it is estimated that 65 percent of the population is Orthodox Christian. This heritage has been a significant factor in the country's politics and has been the glue that bound it tightly to its mighty ally, Russia.

The second largest religious group in Serbia and Montenegro is Muslim, totaling about 19 percent of the population. The rest of the nation's religious groups divide up as follows: 4 percent, Roman Catholics; 1 percent, Protestants, including Baptists, Jehovah's Witnesses, Evangelical Christians, Reformed Christians, Methodists, and Seventh Day Adventists; and 11 percent, others, including Jews, Uniate (or Orthodox) Catholics, and atheists.

The Serbian Orthodox Church

Serbian Orthodoxy has its roots in the city of Constantinople, today known as Istanbul, Turkey, when in the 300s the ancient city's eponym,

Roman emperor Constantine the Great, converted to Christianity. As the centuries progressed, divisions between the Eastern, or Constantinopolitan, Church and the Catholic Church in Rome increased. One major difference between the two churches is that Eastern Orthodox Christians do not believe in the unquestioned authority of the pope in Rome. These differences reached a head in 1054, when the Roman and Constantinopolitan Churches officially split, an occurrence known as the Great Schism.

For their differences, though, the two churches have many common tenets, including the belief in the same seven sacraments: the Eucharist, or Mass; baptism, in which a person is cleansed of sin and officially admitted into the religious community; confirmation, or becoming a spiritual adult; penance, or the confession of sins; holy orders, in which people become religious leaders; marriage; and the anointing of the sick, in which ill persons are blessed to become physically well and receive the grace of the Holy Spirit.

Believers in the Eastern Orthodox denomination of Christianity live mostly in eastern Europe and western Asia; groups tend to be named after their host nation, such as the Russian Orthodox or Greek Orthodox Churches. In Serbia, the branch is called the Serbian Orthodox, while the much smaller branch in Montenegro is called the Montenegrin Orthodox Church.

So how did this part of the world come to adhere mainly to Eastern Orthodoxy? The story begins in the ninth century, when two brothers named Methodius and Cyril converted masses of tribal Slavs to Christianity. To ease the conversion process, the brothers translated the Bible into a regional Slavic language, and Cyril developed a new alphabet based on Greek letters. This Cyrillic alphabet, named after Cyril, is today in wide use in Serbia and Montenegro.

Saint Sava, discussed in chapter 1, deserves much of the credit for converting Serbia to Eastern Orthodoxy. His consecration as the independent archbishop of Serbia in 1219 strengthened the ties between the Serbs and the religious leaders in Constantinople at the expense of those in Rome. The Serbian Orthodox Church especially flourished when in 1346 Serbian emperor Stefan Dušan (1308–55) founded the Serbian Orthodox Church patriarchate, thus establishing the Serbian Orthodox Church as the predominant faith in the southeast Balkans.

On June 5, 2003, citizens of Belgrade commemorated the 600th anniversary of the capital's present name. It was also St. Saviour's Day, named for the patron saint of the city. This Serbian Orthodox Church procession was one of the many activities that celebrated the day. (AP Photo/Mikica Petrović)

Islam

The sizable minority of Muslims in Serbia and Montenegro stems from the prolonged presence of the Ottoman Empire. Islam was founded by the prophet Muhammad in what is now Mecca, Saudi Arabia, in the 600s. Muslims believe in one god, Allah, and their holy book is the Qur'an, or Koran. Muslims practice five pillars of worship: *shahada,* or the acceptance and confirmation of Allah as the one and only God; five daily prayers; almsgiving, or helping the poor; fasting, which Muslims practice from sunrise to sunset every day during the month of Ramadan, the ninth month of the Islamic calendar; and hadj, or pilgrimage, since the Qur'an commands all physically and financially healthy Muslims to make a journey to Mecca.

But while many Bosnian Catholics converted to Islam under the Ottomans, a far smaller number of Serbs did. One reason might have been that many Bosnian Catholics under the Ottomans had roots in

Bogomilism; never having felt comfortable in the Catholic faith, they converted to the newly arrived religion of Islam. Another reason was that Bosnian Catholics had to pay a tax called a *jizya*, levied on most non-Muslims in Islamic empires probably because Catholicism was the religion of most of the Ottomans' enemies. Orthodox Christian Serbs generally did not have to pay the tax. Orthodox Christians were better tolerated than Catholics, so there was not as much of a reason for Orthodox Christians to convert.

Other Religious Communities in Serbia and Montenegro

Islam is the majority religion among ethnic Albanians in Kosovo. However, the vast majority of Kosovan Muslims are not devout. Qemail Morina, head of the highest religious authority in Kosovo, stated, "Alba-

---

TWO NOTABLE RELIGIOUS CHORUSES

Belgrade is home to two of the most highly respected religious singing groups in eastern Europe, both with roots dating to the 19th century.

The older of the two is the First Belgrade Singers' Society, the choir of the Serbian patriarchate and Belgrade Cathedral Church, founded on New Year's Day, 1853. The society has continued in existence uninterrupted into the present. Since 1896 the choir has been singing regularly at Sunday church services and on Orthodox religious holidays, but it is also well known for singing at the coronations of Serbian rulers and installations of Serbian patriarchs. For more than 150 years, the society has sung for royalty from many other nations, too, including such illustrious rulers as Wilhelm II of Germany and Czar Nicholas II of Russia a little more than a century ago. In 1987 it sang in Russia at the 1,000th anniversary of the founding of their Orthodox religion.

The choir's repertoire includes both secular and religious music, encompassing existing classics and its own compositions. While singing in other countries, the society tends to show off Serbian compositions, but in Belgrade the choir expands its selections, rendering everything from Handel's *Messiah* to Mozart's *Requiem*.

nians are not very religious—only 10 percent are practicing Muslims." Most Muslim women do not wear burkas, and the majority walk the streets of Priština in Western-style clothing.

Immediately following the terrorist attacks on the United States on September 11, 2001, which were conducted by militant and fundamentalist Arab Muslims, then Serbian interior minister Dušan Mihailović charged that alleged September 11 mastermind Osama bin Laden's al-Qaeda organization had two bases in Kosovo. However, one officer of the Kosovo Force (KFOR), a NATO-led international force responsible for establishing and maintaining security in Kosovo, responded that he did not believe that there was "an Islamic terrorist threat in Kosovo—there is a high level of security here, and the people are deeply opposed to fundamentalism." Additionally, Kosovo's three leading political figures, including Ibrahim Rugova, are very pro-West, especially since the western member nations in the United Nations and NATO were on their side in the 1999 Kosovo War.

The younger of the two religious chorales is the Baruh Brothers Choir, founded in 1879 as the Serbian-Jewish Singing Society. One historian, Northeastern University professor Joshua Jacobson, reports it as the oldest continually active Jewish singing company in the world. The group changed its name in 1952 in memory of three brothers from the Baruh family, a prominent Jewish Belgrade family, who were killed during World War II.

The choir appears regularly at Serbia's music festivals and has traveled extensively throughout its long history, performing in just about every country in western Europe and in Israel. One of its most noted events was an evening at renowned Carnegie Hall in New York City in 1978.

The ensemble has a huge repertoire, including works by classical composers, such as Haydn, Mozart, and Beethoven, but also contemporary composers, including American Leonard Bernstein. In addition to rendering the works of the world's greatest, the Baruh Brothers Choir enjoys showcasing musical compositions of lesser-known Serbian and Jewish music writers, in all styles. The group has twice been honored by the federal government for its artistic and social achievements and its role as ambassador of Serbia's musical and cultural heritage.

The small percentage of Roman Catholics in the nation fall into two categories: people of Hungarian descent living in Vojvodina, and Croats living in Vojvodina and Montenegro. There is also a very small but active Jewish community.

Until 1492 Jews had lived in thriving communities in Spain. But in 1492 they were expelled from that country during the Spanish Inquisition and were forced to find refuge elsewhere. Many made new homes in eastern Europe, including in the lands of the Ottoman Empire, and it is believed that this is when the first Jews arrived in Belgrade. Roughly 80 percent of Serbia and Montenegro's existing Jewish community in the 1930s was killed by the Ustaša and their fascist sympathizers during World War II.

Judaism, oldest of the world's major religions, was the first to practice monotheism, or belief in one God. Both Christianity and Islam have their bases in Judaism. Jews have two holy books. One is the Bible, especially the first five books, which together are called the Torah and form the basis of all Jewish beliefs. The other is the Talmud, which consists of writings elaborating on Jewish laws and rituals. Unlike Christians, Jews do not accept Jesus as the Messiah and believe that the Messiah has yet to come.

Religion Today in Serbia and Montenegro

Considering that there has been such a troubled recent history of ethnic strife in this region, outsiders may be surprised to learn that Serbia and Montenegro generally have a very tolerant attitude toward people of different religions. While the Serbian Orthodox Church does receive some preferential consideration, there is in fact no state religion. The right to freedom of religion is usually respected by the government.

This right is mostly honored by many members of the clergy, too. In Montenegro, for example, it is common for Orthodox, Muslim, and Catholic communities to share the same city-owned properties for religious services.

That principle of religious tolerance extends to a large degree to Kosovo. The Constitutional Framework for Provisional Self-Government in Kosovo, adopted in May 2001, guarantees freedom of religion in

Kosovo. Similar to those in the rest of the nation, Kosovo's own government officials, as well as the United Nations Interim Mission in Kosovo (UNMIK), have respected this practice.

These views were echoed by several of Kosovo's prominent religious figures. In May 2000 Muslim, Orthodox, and Roman Catholic religious leaders jointly established the Inter-Religious Council of Kosovo, whose purpose is to promote democracy and human rights. At the same time, they issued a declaration that read in part, "With one united voice, we again strongly condemn all acts of violence and all violations of basic human rights. . . . Together we support the building of strong local democratic institutions that will continue to ensure security, peace and well-being for all."

That does not mean, of course, that there have not been acts of religious intolerance in Serbia and Montenegro, but since most citizens of all faiths do not take part in regular organized religious activities, many observers tend to believe these attacks are based on ethnicity rather than religion. Scattered incidents over the past few years in post-Milošević Serbia and Montenegro have included stone throwing, some physical attacks, and even a hand grenade thrown into the yard of a Serb couple living behind a Serbian Orthodox church in Kosovo.

Not all acts of bigotry involved violence. Some consisted of hate speech. Dr. Žarko Gavrilović, an archpriest of the Serbian Orthodox Church who has authored 20 books on the church's history, announced publicly on many occasions that NATO's bombing of Yugoslavia was part of a Jewish-dominated plot to create a new world order. He said of the Jews in general, "Some of them are very good. Moses'[s] people of the Pentateuch [the first five books of the Bible] are very good. But the Talmudic people, they are the Jewish people [who] would like to govern the world." He also said that the Talmud calls for the "crushing of Christianity."

Christian evangelicals from religions such as Baptists and Pentecostals have also been targeted by hate speech. A police inspector named Zoran Luković said in a lecture to Belgrade public school teachers sponsored by the federal Ministry of Education, "Baptists, Pentecostals, and others are dangerous religious cults who damage physical and psychological development of your children. They also destroy families."

Authorities are trying to enforce the laws against violent and hateful acts, although some religious officials have complained about the speed in which police respond. Church authorities are cracking down on clergy members of their own whom they consider to be prejudiced. The largest body of the Serbian Orthodox Church, the Holy Synod, condemned the statements of Gavrilović, and he was suspended from his priestly duties. In Kosovo, UNMIK authorities have provided security at houses of worship and other religious sites to try and guarantee safe worship for all residents.

The Federal Law on Religious Freedom

For some time the government of Serbia and Montenegro has been trying to enact a federal law on religious freedom. While the intent—to ensure that all legitimate religions will have the freedom to worship as they please—may be honorable, some Protestant groups have objected.

According to the draft of the law, those considered the seven traditional religious communities—Serbian Orthodoxy, Islam, Roman Catholicism, the Slovak Evangelical Church, Judaism, the Reform Christian Church, and the Evangelical Christian Church—of the country would automatically be covered. Other groups would have to register with the Federal Ministry for Religious Affairs, who decides whether or not the group should be considered an actual religion covered by the law. While negative decisions on registration would be subject to review by a court, some Protestant denominations have objected to the proposed law, noting that churches not listed would likely be perceived as sects or cults as a result of the ministry's decision. As of early 2003, the law had not yet been passed.

Religion in Schools

Since July 2001 religious education has been mandatory in Serbian public schools. Students are required to attend classes on one of the seven traditional religions listed above. However, students not wishing to take a religious course are given the option of substituting it with a class in civic education. Some parents and clergy have strongly objected to the teaching of religion in schools, advocating a separation of state and religion and fearing that students who choose to take the civic education course will be picked on and ostracized. Yet at the end of 2002, the overwhelming majority of public school students in Serbia and Montenegro have chosen to take the civic education course.

The curricula for the religion courses were designed by leaders of each specific religion. They were then shared with members of the clergy of other religions to make certain that the curriculum did not include any offensive materials. Finally, the course topics were approved by the Serbian Ministry of Education and Sport.

A Religious Dispute in Montenegro

Interestingly, the constitution of Montenegro recognizes the Serbian Orthodox Church but no other religions, including the republic's own Montenegrin Orthodox Church, which is registered simply as a nongovernmental organization (NGO). People who are not Serb Orthodox, including those who are Montenegrin Orthodox, are permitted to worship freely, and the current government of Montenegro is officially noncommittal on the issue.

The Orthodox religious issue has been a hot item among Montenegro's varied political parties. Proindependence parties have advocated that the Montenegrin government officially recognize the Montenegrin Orthodox Church, while pro-Serb parties go so far as to support the establishment of Serb Orthodoxy as the official state religion.

Visiting the Holy Sites

Most of the old cities of Europe have ancient places of worship that are high on travelers' lists of places to visit. But in Belgrade one of the top religious attractions is by European standards almost brand new. The Sveti Marko Orthodox Church is the spiritual heart of Belgrade, and to the uninformed it looks like a relic from several centuries ago. But the church is a copy of a 14th-century Kosovan Church and was built from 1932 to 1940. Its exterior was constructed in the lively Byzantine style, but the interior is decorated in a more somber Orthodox mode. The church suffered some damage from NATO bombings in 1999 and has been undergoing painting and exterior refurbishing. Behind Sveti Marko Orthodox Church is an intriguing little blue and white Russian Orthodox church, which comes as a bonus to visitors.

The most recognizable religious sites in Kosovo are mosques, and among the eight in the town of Peć is the majestic Bajrakli Mosque. The word *bajrakli* translates as "flag," and the mosque is so-called because of the regional tradition of flying a banner on its minaret, or tower, to alert the smaller mosques that the time of day had come to begin saying prayers.

The exact year the Bajrakli Mosque was built is unknown, but it is believed to date to the first few decades of the Ottoman conquest in the second half of the 15th century. The most eye-catching designs of the mosque are the ornamental carvings on the fence, floral ornaments painted on the supporting arches, and the carved floral medallion and symbols of the moon and stars carved into the fountain. While the more than 500-year-old mosque was not directly damaged during the bombing of Kosovo, engineers are concerned that the dropping of the bombs weakened its stability. At the base of the Bajrakli Mosque is a lively street bazaar; this scene makes Peć appear to be a town right out of the Middle East, rather than Europe.

One other notable historic religious site in Peć is the Patrijaršija Monastery, which was a Serbian Orthodox stronghold during the years under the Ottoman Empire. Because of the presence of this monastery during the Ottoman years, the Serb Orthodox were able to keep their religious and ethnic identity, making this an emotional landmark for Serbs today. Inside the monastery are three churches dating from the 13th century with high domes and wonderful medieval frescoes. Just south of Peć is the Visoki Dečani Monastery, raised in 1335 and containing its own medieval frescoes.

The premier religious site in Montenegro is the Monastery of Sveti Petar Cetinjski, known familiarly as the Cetinje Monastery, in the old capital of Cetinje. The first monastery in Cetinje was built by Ivan Crnojević, a ruler from the third Montenegrin dynasty, in 1484. It was destroyed by the Turks in 1692, and the current monastery was constructed in 1785 on the site of a former court of Ivan Crnojević.

The grand, whitish building was the center of regional power, education, and culture in Montenegro, and Montenegro's first elementary and high schools were located in it. It was also here that Prince-Bishop Peter II Petrovich Njegos, an accomplished poet, worked at a printing press and operated a workshop for making zinc cannonballs. The monastery is most highly regarded today for its treasury, which contains a copy of one of the oldest collections of religious songs in the Slavic language. Known as the *Oktoih*, (Book of the Eight Voices), the volume was printed nearby in 1494. The monastery also served as a mausoleum for the Petrović dynasty, and many dukes, princes, bishops, and other monarchs from the family are buried on the property.

NOTES

p. 81 "Serbia and Montenegro has for a long time . . ." "International Religious Freedom Report," Released by the Bureau of Democracy, Human Rights, and Labor. (October 7, 2002) Available on-line. URL: http://www.state.gov/g/drl/rls/irf/2002/13991pf.htm. Downloaded May 13, 2003.

p. 81 "The second largest religious group . . ." "International Religious Freedom Report."

p. 81 "The rest of the nation's religious groups . . ." "International Religious Freedom Report."

pp. 84–85 "Qemail Morina, head . . ." Alexandre Peyrille, "Ethnic Albanians in Kosovo ignore calls to embrace radical Islam," Middle East Times. (September 21, 2001) Available on-line. URL: http://www.metimes.com/2K1/issue2001-38/reg/ethnic_albanians_in.htm. Downloaded July 4, 2003.

p. 85 "However, one officer of the Kosovo Force . . ." Ibid.

p. 87 "At the same time, they issued . . ." Jonathan Luxmoore, "Kosovo Takes a Lesson from Bosnia in Interfaith Relations," Christianity Today. (May 1, 2000) Available on-line. URL: http://www.christianitytoday.com/ct/2000/118/14.0.html. Downloaded May 13, 2003.

p. 87 "He said of the Jews . . ." Frank Brown, "Yugoslav Jews in solidarity with Serb neighbors," Fort Worth Star-Telegram. (May 27, 1999) Available on-line. URL: http://www.star-telegram.com/news/doc/1047/1:RELIGION 51/1:RELIGION 51052799.html. Downloaded May 15, 2003.

p. 87 "A police inspector named . . ." Branko Bjelajac, "Evangelical Churches Stoned, Vandalized," Christianity Today. (July 20, 2001) Available on-line. URL: http://www.christianitytoday.com/global/pf.cgi?/ct/2001/010/16.28.html. Downloaded March 13, 2001.

p. 89 "Yet at the end of . . ." "International Religious Freedom Report," Released by the Bureau of Democracy, Human Rights, and Labor. (October 7, 2002) Available on-line. URL: http://www.state.gov/g/drl/rls/irf/2002/13991pf.htm. Downloaded May 13, 2003.

6

ECONOMY

During the years when the republics of Serbia and Montenegro were part of Yugoslavia, Serbia was economically somewhere in the middle—not as prosperous as Slovenia, but not as poor as Montenegro, which was considered by many to be the backwater of the nation. Today Serbia is still in the midst of trying to finish its transformation from Titoism to a free market economy, as well as trying to recover from both the mismanaged government under Slobodan Milošević and an infrastructure damaged during the Kosovo War. The district of Kosovo is far poorer than the rest of Serbia.

Montenegro, meanwhile, needs economic improvement. Although Montenegro was not directly involved in the civil war from 1991 to 1995, the small republic did suffer financially due to the shrinking of Yugoslav markets and the sanctions imposed by the United Nations. In 1993, for example, two-thirds of the people of Montenegro lived below the poverty level. Montenegro also needs to work on its economic image: It has long had an active black market, which has given the republic a reputation of dishonesty. Businesses in western Europe perceived Montenegro as the place where stolen cars and other pilfered property wound up. Montenegrins used to joke that their national tourist office's slogan should be, "Come to Montenegro—Your Car Is Already There!"

Interestingly, though both republics are part of one nation, each uses a separate currency. Serbia's main unit of currency is the dinar, which was the currency of Yugoslavia. However, Serbia also accepts the euro, used since 1999 by participating European Union countries. Montenegro, meanwhile, accepts only the euro. In July 2003 $1 was equivalent to approximately 57 dinars, and $1 equaled 0.87 euros.

Background

Titoism was not as stringent a form of communism as that which existed in other Eastern European countries. Businesses were under federal control and for the most part were permitted to set their own prices and compete with one another. Titoism was more liberal than the governments in the other Soviet Communist satellites in that workers had some say in their employers' business practices.

However, while those accommodations made Yugoslavia stand out among Eastern European nations, the nation was hardly an example of a free enterprise system. Although Yugoslavia, for the first two decades under Tito, experienced an extended period of economic growth, in time, the nation's republics fell victims to the maladies of other communist-based economies. Mismanagement was the rule in many cases. Politicians and businesspeople did favors for each other based on unwritten and unofficial agreements. Much of the time, factories were built not where manufacturers could make the best use of their resources, but in places where those in office wanted to please constituents. These plants were termed *political factories*.

Factories and other services generally did not make the best use of their employees' abilities. Many employed too many workers, including those with redundant jobs. This lack of efficiency translated into lower profits than the potential promised.

The eastern and southern republics, such as Serbia and Montenegro, were hit harder than Croatia and Slovenia. Economic historians blame the many years that this part of the region was ruled by the Ottoman Empire, which continued as a feudal society well into the 19th century and which was governed by an inefficient and sluggish bureaucracy. Because of that long-standing legacy, little was done to promote the growth of technology and investment.

Montenegro's first factories were not even built until the early 1900s. Soon after the factories, however, came lumber mills, an oil refinery, electric power plants, and a brewery. But until the emergence of Tito as

Yugoslavia's leader after World War II, the main Montenegrin income source continued to be agriculture in what was becoming a rapidly industrialized world. It was not until the postwar era that Montenegro's industrialization grew.

Economy after Titoism

Yugoslavia's high inflation rates and the stagnant growth in the 1970s and early 1980s led to the release of the Krajgher Commission Report in 1983. But the report's recommendations were virtually ignored, increasing the frustration of Yugoslavia's citizens and leading to the eradication of the Titoist system of government in the early 1990s. A drive toward a free market economy was beginning, but the onset of the civil war, which brought with it Slobodan Milošević's inefficient governing style, economic sanctions, NATO bombings in 1999, and a virtual end to the tourist industry, put those goals, once seemingly within reach, on hold. By the time the fighting ended and Milošević was ousted in October 2000, Serbia and Montenegro's national economy in 2000 was half the size it was in 1990.

The new government took action right away to put Serbia and Montenegro on a road to recovery. It put into effect economic stabilization measures and began a strong market reform program. In December 2000 the government renewed its membership in the International Monetary Fund (IMF), an organization consisting of most of the world's nations, which was formed in 1945 to help promote monetary cooperation and foster economic growth among its members. Soon after, Serbia and Montenegro joined two similar groups, the World Bank and the European Bank for Reconstruction and Development (EBRD).

The new memberships have paid off handsomely. A conference sponsored by the World Bank/European Commission in June 2001 raised $1.3 billion for economic restructuring. Further agreements in the fall of 2001 provided debt relief for more than $1 billion owed to creditor governments.

Another organization providing financial assistance to Serbia and Montenegro is the United States Agency for International Development (USAID). A federal government program with roots back to the years immediately following World War II, USAID offers emerging or

---

THE WORLD BANK AND THE EUROPEAN BANK
FOR RECONSTRUCTION AND DEVELOPMENT

The World Bank is one of the world's largest sources of development assistance, especially for those it considers the poorest residents of the poorest nations. It is not a bank in the usual sense, but an organization of the United Nations, which is itself comprised of two smaller groups: the International Bank for Reconstruction and Development (IBRD) and the International Development Association (IDA). Its mission is to provide low-interest loans, interest-free credit, and grants to developing countries, who traditionally cannot borrow money in international markets or can only do so at high interest rates. Recipient nations generally have 35 to 40 years to repay the loans and usually have a 10-year grace period, or time span in which they can repay late loans without a penalty.

Some of the 10,000 professional World Bank employees are also trained to provide basic services to poor and developing nations. These services include building schools and health centers, providing water

---

transitional nations financial assistance that might be used for anything from food to peacekeeping assistance to—in the case of Serbia—rebuilding the nation's infrastructure.

For the two-year period starting with the fall of Milošević in October 2000, USAID's Office of Transition Initiatives (OTI) approved a total of 632 grants worth more than $14 million. The purpose of these grants is to expedite reform in the country, specifically targeting the judiciary branch, economy, local governments, and anticorruption and minority-rights groups. The United States, as well as Western European nations, have placed constant pressure on the Serb-Montenegrin government to fully cooperate with the ICTY; less than full cooperation can mean suspension of financial assistance.

Foreign aid to Serbia and Montenegro totaled more than $1.1 billion in 2000, ranking the nation as one of the primary recipients of foreign aid in the world. Only a handful of other countries, such as Vietnam, China, Egypt, and Poland, have topped the billion-dollar mark in that category. Of the other former republics of Yugoslavia,

and electricity, protecting the environment, and fighting the spread of disease.

The European Bank for Reconstruction and Development (EBRD) was founded in 1991 when Communism was dying in Europe. Former Communist countries like Yugoslavia needed help with the major effort of converting to an economy based on the private sector in a demo-cratic environment. At present, the EBRD is deeply involved in building free market economies and democracies in 27 countries from central Europe to central Asia. Owned by 60 nations and two intergovern-mental institutions, the EBRD is the largest single investor in the region.

The EBRD's main purpose is to provide project financing for both new and existing companies, including banks, industries, and service businesses. Its mandate specifies that it works only in nations that are committed to democratic principles and only with businesses that dis-play a strong respect for the environment. It also stipulates that each EBRD investment must help move a country closer to a free market economy, apply sound banking principles, and only take risks that sup-port private investors, rather than crowding them out.

Bosnia and Herzegovina has received $737 million, Macedonia has received $252 million, Croatia has received $66 million, and Slovenia has received $61 million in 2000.

Proportionately speaking, foreign aid in 2000 totaled a mighty 13.4 percent of Serbia and Montenegro's gross national income (GNI). In comparison, it totaled just 0.3 percent of Slovenia's GNI and only 0.4 percent of Croatia's GNI. This figure is a sound indicator of how depend-ent Serbia and Montenegro is on foreign money.

On May 14, 2002, the executive board of the IMF approved economic aid of roughly $889 million to support Serbia and Montenegro's economic program for the years 2002–05. Whether the nation will receive the full amount of money depends on its overall economic performance. On April 16, 2003, the IMF completed its first annual review of Serbia and Montenegro's performance and gave it full approval, meaning the nation could draw about $137 million right away. A member of the IMF execu-tive board, Anne Krueger, said, "The IMF commends the authorities of Serbia and Montenegro for the impressive further progress in stabilization and reform achieved in 2002." Further payouts will depend on the results of additional reviews.

Serbia and Montenegro is not relying simply on international aid. In the spring and summer of 2001, the nation held the equivalent of a fire sale, selling off some of the country's most valuable businesses, which were still owned by the government. That included three cement plants, a telecommunications business, the national airline, and a company called Zastava, one of eastern Europe's largest arms manufacturers and also the maker of a car called the Yugo. The money was used to pay off companies' foreign debts and compensate pre-1945 owners.

THE YUGO

The jokes came fast, frequently, and furiously. For example:

Question: What is the difference between a Yugo and the principal's office?

Answer: It is less embarrassing if your friends see you leaving the principal's office.

The Yugo, built by Zastava in Kragujevac, is a small, inexpensive car that was introduced in the United States in 1986. Starting at $3,995, the Yugo was meant to fill a need for an economical car in the United States when automobile costs were skyrocketing. By comparison, a small Nissan Sentra started upwards of $7,000 at the time.

It was not long before the Yugo gained a reputation as a total lemon, an unreliable car with little power and which needed constant repair. The American businessman who first imported Yugos, Malcolm Bricklin, stopped importing them in 1992. The civil war in the former Yugoslavia was in full swing, and as a result the Zastava factory stopped production. That made it nearly impossible for American Yugo owners to get their cars repaired. Bricklin's import business went bankrupt.

However, there are devoted Yugo owners who feel the little car got a bad rap. A Virginia man named Tony Underwood and his brother bought 1988 and 1986 Yugos, respectively, and in 2002 they were proud to claim that both their cars were still drivable and that each had more than 100,000 miles on them. Another Yugo owner, Ralph Isenberg of North Carolina, has owned six Yugos and disagrees with those

Where Serbs and Montenegrins Work

Today the nation's economy is diverse, without any single industry or service dominating its gross domestic product (GDP). About 38 percent of the GDP comes from services, about 36 percent from industry, and about 26 percent from agriculture. Most of the country's manufacturing industry is centered in the northern reaches of the country, especially in and around Belgrade. Another important area devoted to industry is in west-central Serbia, extending from the city of Užice, near the border with Bosnia and Herzegovina, eastward to include the cities of Kraljevo and Čačak.

who criticize the car's reliability. He said in 2002, "Treat them right, and they'll work for you."

Malcolm Bricklin is planning to reintroduce Yugos into the United States once more. He says the quality has been improved, but to reflect that upgrade the car will also cost more than it did the first time around. If that is the case, maybe there will be an end to Yugo jokes like this:

Question: How do you double the value of a Yugo?

Answer: Fill the tank with gas.

The little Yugo became synonymous with failure but may be making a comeback. (Photo copyright Pedja Milosavljević)

The autonomous district of Vojvodina is known for its textile factories, but it also contains plants that manufacture metal processing machines, paper, chemical products, and construction material.

Kosovo has few factories, with the exception of some light industry around the capital of Priština and plants processing zinc and tin from the Trepca mines. Montenegro's chief industry is its steel works in Nikšić, while the republic's capital, Podgorica, is home to factories producing agricultural products, such as tobacco. There is a sizable refrigerator plant in Cetinje, Montenegro.

Most of the country's agriculture is based in Vojvodina, thanks to the fertile land that covers nearly 85 percent of its area. About 70 percent of the crops planted in Vojvodina are cereal products. In addition, the lowlands south of the Sava and Danube rivers are also dominated by the planting of grains, especially corn. Upland areas of Serbia are given to orchards, especially plum trees. The highlands are used mostly for animal farming.

Kosovo's farmland is very arable, due in large part to the many small rivers and streams that supply water for irrigation. Many farms in Kosovo are cultivated by their owners for self-sufficiency. The district is also very well known for its vineyards and chestnut, almond, and fruit trees and cattle breeding. While Montenegro's economy was long dominated by agriculture, the republic's terrain is not generally arable. Only about 10 percent of the land is farmed, and about 40 percent of that is devoted to the growing of grains. Sheep farming provides income to some residents of Montenegro's hillier areas.

Montenegro's seacoast is once again drawing tourists, especially sun worshippers who come to enjoy the Mediterranean-style climate. Sveti Stefan, once a tiny fishing village, has been transformed into a luxury resort town. The ancient city of Budva is also a popular beach resort, as well as a destination for those wanting to explore ancient history.

Kosovo has been trying to promote its medieval monasteries and forts for tourists, but most outsiders still associate the district with war and devastation. While Vojvodina does not have a coastline, its rivers and lakes draw tourists seeking aquatic recreation. Serbia proper promotes its Orthodox monasteries for history lovers and its more than 50 mineral springs for seekers of pleasure and good health.

Poverty

While improvements in Serbia and Montenegro's standards of living are being made, the nation still suffers from the fallout of war, sanctions, and nearly five decades of Communist rule. A total of 30 percent of the nation's people live below the poverty level. The level of poverty in Kosovo alone has been estimated at from 30 percent to 50 percent. The estimated rate of inflation in 2002 was 18 percent, and the official unemployment rate was an extraordinarily high 28 percent.

However, that may be an overestimation of the total unemployment in Serbia and Montenegro. The country, like the other former Yugoslavia republics, has a strong underground economy, also known as the gray, or shadow, economy. Some profitable businesses do not register with the government, so that they can avoid paying what some consider unfairly high taxes. In addition, unregistered businesses can avoid complying with government regulations, which can also save on expenses.

People who are employed by these gray market companies do not show up in official unemployment statistics. Yet even if many Serbs and Montenegrins are working with unregistered businesses, the unemployment figure would still reach well into the teens, which is high by any standards.

A small child begs for money in Priština, Kosovo, in front of an election poster promising a "better Priština" for the future, just before October 2002 elections. (AP Photo/Visar Kryeziu)

NOTES

p. 93 "In 1993, for example . . ." "Economic Development of Montenegro," Montenet. Available on-line. URL: http://www.montenet.org/econ/ecdevel.htm. Downloaded June 7, 2003.

p. 93 "Montenegrins used to joke . . ." Dusan Stojanovic, "Montenegro: A breathtaking Balkan diamond in the rough," Pittsburgh Tribune-Review. (June 8, 2003) Available on-line. URL: http://www.pittsburghlive.com/x/tribune-review/entertainment/travel/s_138284.html. Downloaded June 8, 2003.

p. 95 "By the time the fighting ended . . ." "Serbia and Montenegro," World Factbook 2002, CIA. (March 19, 2003) Available on-line. URL: http://www.cia.gov/cia/publications/factbook/geos/yi.html. Downloaded May 29, 2003.

p. 96 "For the two-year period starting . . ." "Field Report: Serbia & Montenegro, October 2002," USAID. Available on-line. URL: http://www.usaid.gov/hum_response/oti/country/serb/rpt1002.html. Downloaded June 8, 2003.

p. 96 "Foreign aid to Serbia and Montenegro . . ." "Serbia and Montenegro Data Profile," World Bank. Available on-line. URL: http://devdata.worldbank.org/external/CPProfile.asp?Selected Country. Downloaded June 5, 2003.

p. 96 "Only a handful of other . . ." "Serbia and Montenegro Data Profile."

pp. 96–97 "Of the former republics . . ." "Serbia and Montenegro Data Profile."

p. 97 "Proportionately speaking, foreign aid in 2000, . . ." "Serbia and Montenegro Data Profile."

p. 97 "In comparison, it totaled . . ." "Serbia and Montenegro Data Profile."

pp. 97–98 "A member of the IMF executive board . . ." "IMF Approves US $137 Million Credit Disbursement Under Extended Arrangement with Serbia and Montenegro," IMF. (April 16, 2003) Available on-line. URL: http://www.imf.org/external/np/sec/pr/2003/pr0351.htm. Downloaded May 30, 2003.

p. 99 "He said in 2002 . . ." David Kiley, "Entrepreneur plans U.S. comeback for the Yugo," USA Today. (May 9, 2002) Available on-line. URL: http://www.usatoday.com/money/autos/2002/05/10/yugo-return.htm. Downloaded June 7, 2003.

p. 101 "A total of 30 percent . . ." "Serbia and Montenegro," World Factbook 2002, CIA. (March 19, 2003) Available on-line. URL: http://www.cia.gov/cia/publications/factbook/geos/yi.html. Downloaded May 29, 2003.

p. 101 "The level of poverty in Kosovo . . ." "Qualitative Poverty Survey Project," United Nations Development Programme. Available on-line. URL: http://www.kosovo.undp.org/Projects/QQPS/qqps.htm. Downloaded June 9, 2003.

p. 101 "The estimated rate of inflation . . ." "Serbia and Montenegro," World Factbook 2002, CIA. (March 19, 2003) Available on-line. URL: http://www.cia.gov/cia/publications/factbook/geos/yi.html. Downloaded May 29, 2003.

7

CULTURE

The heritage of Serbia and Montenegro goes back centuries, and during that time people here have had innumerable interactions with other cultures. Influences from the Turks; central Europeans, such as the Hungarians; eastern Europeans, including the Bulgarians; and small but active ethnic groups like the Roma, or Gypsies, have affected the way Serbs have manifested their feelings in music, painting, literature, and other arts. Much of the manner in which the nation's artists exhibit their views depends on what part of Serbia and Montenegro they call home.

Music

Serbian and Montenegrin folk music is traditionally vibrant and lively. The music of Vojvodina and Serbia proper is dominated by a variety of instruments, including the accordion, the violin, a shepherd's flute known as a *frula*, and two types of bagpipes, both made from goatskin: small ones called *caraba*, and larger ones known as *gajde*. The better known Scottish bagpipe, on the other hand, is traditionally made from sheepskin. Serbian and Montenegrin bagpipe music is similar to that of neighboring Bulgaria.

Ethnic Albanians in Kosovo lean toward folk music dominated by the high-pitched, rambling, fairly whiny sound of a flute called a *zurna*, holdover from the Ottoman days and a popular instrument in many Arab countries. In Montenegro the national folk instrument has for centuries been a crude type of violin, which in the United States might be referred to as a fiddle. In Montenegro it is called a *gusle*.

The *tamburica,* also known as the tamburitza, a stringed instrument similar to a lute, has long been a mainstay of Balkan folk music, especially among Croatians and Bosnians. It is crafted in varying sizes and is played as either a solo instrument or as an accompaniment to singers. The *tamburica* is played by Serbs and Montenegrins also, but it is not as dominant here as it is in those other south Slavic cultures. It likely dates to the 14th century and has similarities to the Italian mandolin and the Russian balalaika.

Serbs generally play the *tamburica* in a different manner than Bosnians and Croatians. With the occasional addition of a violin and accordion, Serbs use the *tamburica* to play a fast, furious, and rambunctious Roma-style music. It is especially popular in Vojvodina, particularly in the city of Novi Sad, regarded as Vojvodina's cultural capital.

Blehmuzika

The local word for brass music is *blehmuzika,* and according to many historians and entertainment critics, it can be described as the national music of Serbia and Montenegro. Its roots range from the basic beats of Turkish military bands to the exotic melodies of Roma folk. *Blehmuzika*'s genesis is believed to date back two centuries, but it is as popular today as ever.

The dominant instrument in *blehmuzika* is the trumpet, introduced to the Balkans when the land was under the control of the Ottomans. Turkish soldiers used the instrument as a tool for communication, and in time it was picked up by the Roma. *Blehmuzika*'s birth has been dated to the Karageorge uprising of 1805, when Roma brass bands introduced the trumpet into Serbia.

Today there are two main forms of *blehmuzika.* One is a more traditional bouncy, melodic dance style played in western Serbia. The other is a more raucous, improvisational version, played mostly in southern Serbia and mainly by Roma. The energetic Roma version seems to be more popular commercially, and Roma *blehmuzika* musicians are in frequent demand for celebrations. Attending a big Serbian wedding today means almost certainly getting the chance to hear entertainment by a *blehmuzika* band.

Music critics have accepted *blehmuzika* as a legitimate form of jazz. In fact, highly regarded jazz musicians have praised this style of Serbian music. Frank London, a noted jazz and klezmer performer who has played with the likes of David Byrne of Talking Heads and rap artist LL Cool J, referred to *blehmuzika* as "the unmistakable essence of funk." Jazz legend, trumpet player Miles Davis, upon hearing the music performed live, reacted in a stunned manner and exclaimed, "I didn't know you could play the trumpet that way."

Like all living musical styles, *blehmuzika* is in a constant state of evolution. One Roma trumpet player explained, "Most of the new tunes have an almost disco rhythm. They're made to listen to in clubs, for younger and urban audiences." The latest and the greatest Serbian brass bands gather every August in a sports field in the town of Guča, about 100 miles south of Belgrade, for a three-day festival that doubles as a rollicking party ruled by music, food, drinking, and dancing. It must seem like an invasion for the 2,000 full-time residents of Guča when the festival takes place, since about 100,000 to 250,000 festival-goers arrive in town for the event, which has been an annual happening since 1960. A fan who attended a recent Guča festival commented, "When I go to

One of Serbia and Montenegro's many blehmuzika *bands entertains during a folk festival.* (Photo copyright Pedja Milosavljević)

bed at night my body shakes with the rhythm for at least another half an hour."

Former Yugoslav president Slobodan Milošević was accused of hijacking the music during his years in office and making it a political symbol of Serb nationalism. Festival promoter Ilija Stanković said, "It was manipulated" by Milošević. Stanković added, "But the most exciting thing about the history of the festival is that a political speech has never taken place on the stage of Guča. It is the people's festival."

The Kolo

It is common at the Guča Festival to see audience members spontaneously stand, join hands, and dance in a circle. This round dance is the kolo, and while the word *kolo* is the Croatian word "wheel" and some cultural historians believe the dance may have originated in Croatia, it is today viewed as Serbia's national dance. The circle formed by the dancers represents the circular shape of the sun.

In its early forms in the 19th century, the kolo was often accompanied by bagpipes and *frula*, and until the onset of World War II it was a mandatory dance at the Serbian court. But by the end of the war, the bagpipe had mostly been replaced by the merry sound of the accordion, and the use of the *frula* was continued mainly as a symbol of Serbian national identity.

There are many variations of the kolo, based on the directions the dancers move, the steps they perform, and the basic rhythm. One of the more unusual versions, in which the dancers move in the opposite direction of the most common kolos, is known as *mrtvačko kolo*, literally "kolo for the dead." The kolo is danced mostly at parties nowadays.

Yu-Rock

Yu-Rock is a shortened term for Yugoslavian rock and roll, and it has been around longer than many might think. In the late 1950s, Yugoslav teenagers listening to western European based radio stations, such as Radio Luxembourg and the Voice of America, first heard the sounds of American rock-and-roll pioneers such as Elvis Presley, Jerry Lee Lewis, and Little Richard, as well as the British band the Shadows. Young musicians in Yugoslavia began playing the songs of Presley, Lewis, and the rest, but they faced a problem American and British teens did not have to worry about: Electric instruments were hard to come by in Yugoslavia, so the first Yugoslavian rock concerts were performed by musicians playing acoustic guitars. Some improvised with fake electric guitars made by fitting homemade pickups, usually small microphones, inside the bodies of acoustic guitars and using radios as amplifiers.

By the early 1960s, real electric guitars could be purchased in the stores of Belgrade, and aspiring rock musicians took advantage of their availability. As early as 1962, Belgrade had its own superstar bands, including Zlatni Dečaci (Golden Boys) and Siluete (Silhouette), who had legions of young female fans. Shockingly to many, the Titoist leadership did little to stifle the popularity of rock and roll, and by the end of the 1960s British bands, such as the Beatles and the Rolling Stones, American bands, including the Beach Boys, and African-American soul music singers like Aretha Franklin, Wilson Pickett, and Otis Redding could be heard all over Yugoslavia. One Belgrade band, Elipse, was very popular at home for its soul-influenced music. Serbian-based groups

The kolo, performed in a circle, is Serbia and Montenegro's national dance.
(Courtesy Free Library of Philadelphia)

BORA DJORDJEVIĆ

Šabac is a town located on the Danube River west of Belgrade and just across the border of Vojvodina. The people of Šabac have become best known for a heroic act in 1940, when many risked their lives to save 1,300 Jewish civilians from the Nazis and Ustaša.

Since then Šabac has also become regarded as the birthplace of one of Serbia and Montenegro's best-known rock stars. Bora Djordjević was born in 1953 but became known across Yugoslavia in 1979 as the angry young lead singer of the pioneering Yugoslav punk rock band Riblja Čorba. With shoulder-length blonde hair framing his face, Djordjević spewed out biting, confrontational, and sometimes vulgar lyrics that took on the Communist leadership. He was proud to make waves and shock his listeners, and Riblja Čorba's records became best sellers in Yugoslavia.

When Slobodan Milošević first became prominent in 1987, Djordjević initially supported the Serb leader for his pride in Serbian nationhood. But evidence of Serb genocide organized by Milošević caused Djordjević to change his views. By the mid-1990s, Djordjević, now a solo act, his hair more gray than blonde and sporting a salt-and-

lagged behind in popularity in the early mid-1970s to bands such as Bosnian hard rockers Bijelo Dugme (White Button), but by the late 1970s there was rebellion in the musical world of Yugoslavian rock.

Punk and new wave music may have originated on the streets of London and New York City, but it hit Yugoslavia in 1978, a bit earlier than most other European countries. Punk bands emerged from many of Yugoslavia's big cities, and Belgrade's contributions to this new genre of rock music were Partibrejkers (Gate Crashers), Šarlo Akrobata (Charles the Acrobat), Električni Orgazam (Electric Orgasm) and perhaps the biggest of all, Riblja Čorba (Fish Soup), featuring lead singer Bora Djordjević. Prior to the onset of the punk movement, most Yugoslav songs were about romance. But Djordjević and his contemporaries took on political issues, such as repression and freedom. One music critic described Djordjević's lyrics as "a chronicle of the dark side of life in real existing Socialism."

pepper beard and a pot belly, had become one of the most vocal opponents of Milošević and his wife, Mirjana Marković.

In the winter of 1996–97 one of the most popular songs in Serbia was a stinging anti-Marković tune performed by Djordjević and titled, "Grandma Jula." The song's title came from Marković's role as head of the political party Yugoslav United Left (JUL). At a January 16, 1997, Belgrade concert, Djordjević told the audience to roars of approval, "We don't need children's stories about fairy-tale witches. We all have Grandma Jula."Noted Serb rock musician Momčilo Bajagić proclaimed that Grandma Jula was "the anthem of the protest movement. Everyone knows the words by heart."

Djordjević's bold song made him enemies. He received death threats, he was banned from radio and television performances, and legitimate record stores would not carry his song, forcing fans to purchase it from not-always-reliable street vendors.

Djordjević was onstage singing at a concert in Milošević's hometown of Požarevac in October 2000 when word came that Milošević conceded defeat. He interrupted his music to announce, "I came to free Požarevac after 10 years and it is I who has the honor to let you know that Milošević has admitted that he lost." The audience cheered wildly.

Yugoslavia was recognized throughout the 1980s as home to one of the most creative rock music scenes in Europe. One of Belgrade's clubs, Akademija, was considered by the British media as one of the finest in Europe. But when the war started in June 1991 and the country of Yugoslavia fell apart, the media, the clubs, and record companies, which had relied on interrepublic cooperation, also fell apart. That, in turn, meant that many of the music groups, without a strong infrastructure of support, lost their markets and disbanded. This included Riblja Čorba.

There were exceptions. In the spring of 1992, the bands Električni Orgazam, Partibrejkers, and a Belgrade group, Ekatarina Velika (Katherine the Great) pooled their resources and formed a super group they called Rimtutituki. They recorded an antiwar song called "Mir, Brate, Mir" (peace, brother, peace), which became a big hit that year. During the war, many Serbian rock musicians left the republic, while those who stayed mainly favored antiwar rock anthems.

A milestone in the Serbian and Montenegrin rock scene occurred on June 19, 1998, when a Belgrade musician named Antonje Pusić, singing under the stage name Rambo Amadeus, became the first Serbian rock musician since 1991 to play in Sarajevo. In addition to building bridges, the antiwar performer proved to other Serbian musicians that it was not dangerous for Serbs to play in Sarajevo. That same year Sarajevo band Indeksi played in the Montenegrin towns of Nikšić and Podgorica and also in Belgrade.

Since then, many rock bands have played in cities in the other Yugoslav republics. Some bands, which were just starting out when the war began, have had a chance to tour the new Yugoslav countries and garner followings. Belgrade music fans are welcoming these bands as if the war never happened. One Belgrade rock critic, Petar Janjatović, said in the winter of 2001, "I guess that what happened to the Serbian Rock scene in the course of the last 10 years, is much better than we deserved. Indeed, a very lively rock and roll scene emerged from the years of war."

Art

The earliest art on view in Serbia and Montenegro today can be seen in the forms of clay dishes and figures and ritual vases which date to prehistory, many discovered in tombs and remnants of settlements dating to about 1600 B.C. But among the oldest Slavic-influenced art in the country today are frescoes painted in the 900s on the walls of Serbia's Petrova Church. Still recognizable are five scenes depicting the life of Jesus Christ.

Over the next several centuries, most art created here reflected spiritual life, whether as paintings or architecture. On display in the National Museum in Belgrade is a brightly illuminated biblical text dating to 1190 and known as Miroslav's Gospel. Created in medieval Zeta, now Montenegro, it is believed to be one of the oldest Cyrillic manuscripts on record, and museum-goers are amazed by its ornate and colorful illustrations. Also exhibited from the medieval era are fragments of frescoes from 12th- to 15th-century monasteries. The art not related to religion mainly consists of gold and silver jewelry and wood carvings once the property of royalty.

Much of the area's art produced over the next few centuries ranged from medieval, religious-themed work to pieces that show the borrowing of ideas spawned in northern Greece.

Influences from Germany and Austria had a large effect on Serbian and Montenegrin painting in the 18th and 19th centuries. By the mid-1800s, Serbia's best artists included romanticists Djura Jaksić and Novak Radonjić and realists Djordje Krstić and Uroš Predić. Serbia's first woman painter to become accepted for her art was Katarina Ivanović (1817–82). The impressionistic movement which swept Paris, France, in the late 1800s was a huge influence on Serbia's painters, and Paris continued to motivate Serbian and Montenegrin artists well into the first few decades of the 1900s.

Regarded as one of the most outstanding 20th-century artists from that period was a native of Cetinje, Montenegro, named Petar Lubarda (1907–74) who studied art in Paris in the late 1920s. Lubarda's modernist oil on canvas, *A Night in Montenegro*, which he created in 1951, is one of his best known.

Naïve Art

Naïve art is likely the most defining artistic movement of the 20th century in Serbia and Montenegro. It was born in the early 1930s, and many art historians say it made its public debut not in Serbia or Montenegro but in Croatia, when on September 13, 1931, a colony of peasant painters known as the Zemlja (ground, or soil) opened an exhibition at the Art Pavilion in Zagreb.

Regardless of who exhibited the first example of naïve art on canvas, by 1933, Serbia's Janko Brašić (1906–94), a native of the village of Oparić, was painting in the realistic, basic, primitive and folk-dominated style which became known as naïve art. After decades of Parisian-oriented impressionism, as well as expressionism and abstract art produced in the Balkans, this homegrown Slavic style proved fresh and original and could be appreciated by all. Brašić created everything from paintings to frescoes to sculptures, and his subjects represented the everyday lives of hard-working Serbs: farm labor, such as harvesting crops and mowing fields; ritual feasts, customs, and traditions; and people simply out for a relaxing stroll in the park.

A trio of Serbian artists, Milan Rasić (b. 1931), Miloslav Jovanović (b. 1935), and Dušan Jevtović (b. 1925) first appeared in the 1960s and brought widespread recognition to naïve art. Rasić emphasized the lives of peasants in serene settings, Jovanović based his work in dreamlike

A prime example of Yugoslav naïve art is "St. Eliah the Thunderer" by Ilija Bosilj.
(Courtesy Free Library of Philadelphia)

tableau, and Jevtović celebrated Serbian life in his works, such as *A Harvest* (1969), *Winter Weddings* (1983), and *Summer in My Village* (1986), with busy and idealized country settings and the hilly backgrounds he recalled from his childhood in the village of Gornja Trnava. The three artists are still active today.

Naïve art is recognized in Serbia as such a native art form that it is celebrated in the Museum of Naïve Art in the town of Jagodina, a specialty museum devoted solely to this genre and founded in 1960. The museum's permanent collection has about 2,500 works, including paintings, sculptures, graphics, and drawings, by 276 painters and sculptors.

Literature

Most, but not all, of the earliest examples of pure Serbian and Montenegrin literature are church-related. Among the earliest recorded Serbian authors are members of the Nemanja dynasty, including Saint Sava and Stefan Prvovenčani, who wrote biographies of Orthodox religious leaders, such as archbishops, and of Serbian kings in the 12th and 13th centuries. Beginning in the late 17th century, Serbian literature was in a lull, with people spending their energies not creating new works but copying old ones.

A new Serbian age began about 100 years later with the emergence of Vuk Stefanović Karadžić (1787–1864), an illustrious lexicographer who collected and published Serbia's folktales in numerous volumes. Karadžić also wrote the first Serbian dictionary in 1818 and is regarded as the creator of the modern Serbian alphabet, which he crafted by reforming the existing Cyrillic alphabet. Karadžić's crowning achievement was a translation of the New Testament in 1847, which he followed with a translation of the Old Testament with the assistance of a younger associate named Djuro Daničić (1825–82).

One of the heroic Serbian folk poems written by Karadžić told the tale of the famed Battle of Kosovo Polje. It is regarded by many critics as the finest example of Serbian folk poetry.

> Has the hour arrived for us to journey
> To the level plain of Kosovo
> And join forces with the noble Tsar?
> My son, you will remember that grave oath—
> Lazarus exhorted us like this:
> 'Whoever is a Serb, of Serbian blood,
> Whoever shares with me this heritage,
> And he comes not to fight at Kosovo,
> May he never have the progeny
> His heart desires, neither son nor daughter;
> Beneath his hand let nothing decent grow—
> Neither purple grapes nor wholesome wheat;
> Let him rust away like dripping iron
> Until his name shall be extinguished!'
> Then Musich Stefan rests upon soft pillows
> While Vaistina his friend and loyal servant
> Eats his meal, drinks his share of wine,
> And goes to walk before the lordly castle.
> He looks into the clear transparent skies
> And sees the moon—bright and in the west;
> The morning star is rising in the east.

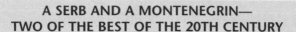

A SERB AND A MONTENEGRIN—
TWO OF THE BEST OF THE 20TH CENTURY

Genetics likely had a major role in Milorad Pavić's life's calling. He was born in 1929 to a respected family of writers in Belgrade. Or, as Pavić himself wrote, "I have been a writer for two hundred years now. Long ago, in 1766, a Pavić published a collection of poems in Budim and we have considered ourselves a family of writers ever since."

Pavić graduated from the University of Belgrade, then received a Ph.D. in literary history at the University of Zagreb. He taught for a while at different universities, including those in the Serbian cities of Belgrade and Novi Sad, but he settled down to writing full-time in the mid-1960s. His first published work was a collection of poetry that came out in 1967. Early on he also published scholarly works called monographs about different types of literary history.

In 1984 Pavić published his first novel, a playful history of a fictional people he called the Khazars, who lived somewhere in the Slavic region of Europe between the seventh and ninth centuries. The book, *Dictionary of the Khazars,* tells the story of the Khazars according to three different points of view: from the Christians, the Jews, and the Muslims, the theme being that there is no absolutely correct answer to any basic question. The book was a best-seller and received great reviews. Critics compared it to other classics about imaginary places, including Jonathan Swifts's *Gulliver's Travels;* Lewis Carroll's *Alice in Wonderland,* and L. Frank Baum's *The Wizard of Oz.*

An introductory excerpt reads, "The Khazars, and the Khazar state, vanished from the stage of history as a result of the event that is the main concern of this book—their conversion from their original faith, unknown to us today, to one (again, it is not known which) of three known religions of the past and present—Judaism, Islam, or Christianity. The collapse of the Khazar Empire followed soon after their conversion. A Russian military commander of the 10th century, Prince Svyatoslav, gobbled up the Khazar Empire like an apple, without even dismounting from his horse."

Pavić followed *Dictionary of the Khazars* with more novels that use metaphors and playful language to explore basic questions of life, such as what is truth? Being a Serb weighs heavily on Pavić's mind. He wrote after the Kosovo War, "I have not killed anyone. But they have killed me. Long before my death. It would have been better for my books had their author been a Turk or a German. I was the best known writer of the most hated nation in the world—the Serbian nation. XXI century started for me avant la date 1999 when NATO air forces bombed Belgrade and Serbia. Since that moment the river Danube on whose banks I was born is not navigable. I think God graced me with infinite favor by granting me the joy of writing, and punished me in equal measure, precisely because of that joy perhaps."

Esteemed writer Danilo Kiš was born in 1935 in Vojvodina. He says he was born in Novi Sad, although some biographies claim Kiš was born in the town of Subotica, near the Hungarian border. His father was a Hungarian Jew, but his mother was a Montenegrin, so Montenegrins proudly consider him to be one of their own. As a young man, he studied literature in Belgrade, though he spent much of the rest of his life in Paris, France.

Many members of Kiš's family died during the Holocaust of World War II, so it makes sense that much of Kiš's creative output focuses on wartime persecution of innocent people, especially, though not always, Jews. One of his novels, *Garden, Ashes,* tells the tale of a boy named Andi Scham in his early teens, who spends World War II on the run from persecution and in search of his missing father.

Kiš told an interviewer in 1984 that the character of Eduard Scham, the father in the book, is based on his father. Kiš admitted, "The father became more idealized because I knew him so little; he was often away. My own father died at Auschwitz in 1944. He became mythical to me when I realized that he had an exceptional destiny and that my own destiny was marked by his Jewishness. I kept my father's documents during the war with an idea—a very clear idea, I would say now—that one day these documents and these letters would become part of my literature. The long letter which is reproduced at the end of *Hourglass* showed me that my father was something of a writer manqué. I knew my father so vaguely that I was able to use certain facts to transform an ordinary Central European man into a mythical character; I could assign him certain of my own ideas."

One of Kiš's most highly regarded books was about oppression under the Stalinist Soviet Union. Titled *A Tomb for Boris Davidovich,* the book presents seven stories based on historic fact but which are fictionalized by Kiš. In each, the main characters, including title character Boris Davidovich, all die, a dark commentary by Kiš on the oppression of Stalinist Communism. Kiš received praise for his use of images.

In addition to novels, Kiš also wrote plays and short stories. He died prematurely of cancer at the age of 54 in 1989.

The hour has thus arrived for them to journey
To the level plain of Kosovo
And join forces with the noble Tsar.

In Montenegro, the literary movement began later than that in Serbia, in part because the Montenegrins, who seemed to be in a perpetual struggle for survival, have been more concerned with trying to stay alive through the centuries than writing works of literature. For a long time the basic form of artistic and literary expression in Montenegro was epic poetry sung and accompanied by a gusle. Orthodox religious leaders are regarded as the founders of Montenegro's literature, and the person accepted as the author of the first such work was Bishop Vasilije Petrović, whose *History of Montenegro* was published in 1754. Literary historians today describe it as more of a political manifesto than pure history.

Modern Literature

The mid-18th century is regarded as a period of enlightenment in Serbian literature, and the individual often referred to as the first modern Serbian writer, Dositej Obradović (1739–1811), emerged from the beginning of that period. Obradović began his career as a monk, then traveled through much of Europe, first in the Balkans, then in the west. He spent his time familiarizing himself with the cultures and languages of others. Obradović is credited with creating a literary culture in the Serbian vernacular. He also founded Serbia's first institute for advanced schooling and influenced a stream of other 19th-century Serbian writers.

By the late 19th and early 20th centuries, Serbian and Montenegrin literature was as respected as that of any people. One of Serbia's most renown poets from that period was Ljubomir Nedić (1858–1902), who emphasized aesthetics and beauty in his work. Among the most famous Montenegrin authors of the 20th century were Borislav Pekić (1930–92), a novelist known for putting touches of irony in his books, and Miodrag Bulatović (1930–91), admired for his brilliant imagination in novels such as *Hero on a Donkey* and *People with Four Fingers*.

To pick the most popular or best-regarded modern authors in Serbia and Montenegro would stir a major debate, but it is safe to assume that Milorad Pavić and Danilo Kiš would be on most of the lists.

NOTES

p. 105 "Frank London, a noted . . ." "Serbian Burning Brass Sets Miles' Ears on Fire." Available on-line. URL: http://www.rockpaperscissors.biz/index.cfm/fuseaction/current.press_release/project_id/29.cfm. Downloaded May 16, 2003.

p. 105 "Jazz legend, trumpet player Miles Davis . . ." Ibid.

p. 105 "One Roma trumpet player . . ." Andrew Gray, "Bold as Brass, Serbs Celebrate Trumpet Tradition," Reuters. (August 17, 2002) Available on-line. URL: http://www.balkanpeace.org/hed/archive/aug02/hed5149.shtml. Downloaded May 16, 2003.

pp. 105–106 "A fan who attended . . ." "Serbian trumpets blast down cultural barriers," Agence France-Presse. (August 14, 2002) Available on-line. URL: http://www.invest-in-serbia.com/tws/belgrade/info03.htm. Downloaded May 16, 2003.

p. 106 "Festival promoter Ilija Stanković . . ." Ibid.

p. 108 "One music critic . . ." Rudiger Rossig, "Yu-Rock: A Brief History: No Problems in my neighborhood: Punk, New Wave and the eighties in SFRJ." Available on-line. URL: http://www.klikeri.co.yu/tajnigrad/rossig.html. Downloaded May 18, 2003.

p. 109 "At a January 16, 1997, Belgrade concert . . ." Chris Hedges, "A Rock Singer's Raucous Role: Serbia's Jeer Leader," New York Times, January 17, 1997.

p. 109 "Noted Serb rock musician . . ." Ibid.

p. 109 "He interrupted his music to announce . . ." "Explosion of joy in Belgrade and Serbia after Milošević concedes," Agence France-Presse. (October 7, 2000) Available on-line. URL: http://www.balkanpeace.org/hed/archive/oct00/hed818.shtml. Downloaded May 18, 2003.

p. 110 "One Belgrade rock critic . . ." Rossig.

p. 112 "The museum's permanent collection . . ." "Collection," Museum of Naive Art website. (April 10, 2003) Available on-line. URL: http://www.naiveart.org.yu/zbirkae.htm. Downloaded May 23, 2003.

pp. 113, 116 "One of the heroic Serbian folk poems . . ." "The Battle of Kosovo," translated by John Matthias and Vladeta Vuckovic, Balkania.net. Available on-line. URL: http://www.members.tripod.com/Balkania/resources/history/battle_of_kosovo.html. Downloaded May 23, 2003.

p. 114 "'I have been a writer . . .'" Milorad Pavić, "Autobiography." Available on-line. URL: http://www.khazars.com/autobiography.html. Downloaded May 23, 2003.

p. 114 "'The Khazars, and the . . .'" Milorad Pavić, Dictionary of the Khazars. New York: Vintage Books, 1989, p. 2.

pp. 114–115 "He wrote after the Kosovo War . . ." Pavić, "Autobiography."

p. 115 "Kís admitted . . ." Brendan Lemon, "An Interview with Danilo Kís," Dalkey Archive Press. Available on-line. URL: http://www.centerforbookculture.org/interviews/interview_kis.html. Downloaded May 24, 2003.

8

DAILY LIFE

With a democratic government in power and the civil war in the past, the citizens of Serbia and Montenegro are doing their best to return to normal life. Unlike in Bosnia and Herzegovina, the people here do not need to spend most of their efforts trying to physically rebuild their country. However, some would say they—especially the Serbs—are making a concerted effort to rebuild something that will take just as much time and work: their public image.

A young Serbian woman, Goga, wrote of her contradictory feelings on a website called VirtualTourist.com, on which people discuss their countries and recommend places to visit. Goga introduced her nation, once known as Yugoslavia, in the following way:

> For some people it was happy country, for some it was bad. . . . But it was my country. A country I loved as a child, and things you love when you are child you hardly forget. The way I remember it, is like it was happy place, nice people, free, safe. Where ever you go . . . all over ex Yu [sic]. That is how my childhood was, HAPPY. And then something went wrong. It was all gone in just second. It lasted longer, but when you are young and you don't understand it, it is just confusing and scary. Then I lived in FRY [Federative Republic of Yugoslavia], [which] consisted of Serbia and Montenegro. And now I live in Serbia and Montenegro. I don't know what to say about all that, it makes you wonder who you are and where you do come from in fact. Anyway I don't want to sound pathetic.

Goga encouraged Internet users to read the rest of her comments about the land she loves. But she concluded her written introduction with the following sentence, all the words underscored: "I just want people with hate in their hearts to leave my pages right now (and leave no trace of being here)."

Life goes on in Serbia and Montenegro. People host parties, go to school and work, celebrate holidays, enjoy a home-cooked meal that nobody outside Serbia and Montenegro could ever make to perfection, and spend their spare time checking out the latest movie or playing basketball on a playground. More than anything, Serbs and Montenegrins want others to know that their nation is not behind the times or dangerous.

A Serbian teenager named Erik who now lives with his family in Canada, also hosts a page on VirtualTourist.com. He was struck by how little North Americans know about his country: "When I went to Canada for the first time, many people asked me[,] do we have a TV in Yugoslavia? The answer is yes, we do have coloured TVs, computers (Yes, we're trying to be as western as we can), telephones or whatsoever in Yugoslavia! Yugoslavia might not be as poor as people think it is. There are many modern things in our lives."

Family and Home Life

Serbs and Montenegrins tend to be more reserved with strangers than Americans are, but they are friendly and helpful once they get better acquainted with individuals. People greet friends by shaking hands and acknowledging each other with phrases such as, "Dobro jutro" (good morning), "Dobar dan," (good day), and "Dobro veče" (good evening). They may greet close friends or family members with three kisses on the cheek. It is an accepted custom that a guest greets a host, a younger person greets an elder, a rider greets a pedestrian, and a man greets a woman.

While men and women have equal rights within the law, women have always tended to be the backbone of the household. In rural areas, there were times when women took over the operations of entire farms, most often if men were away on business or at war. In earlier days, Serbs lived in *zadruga*, or large family communities, but today the family unit is very much as it is in the United States and western Europe, with two parents, one or two children, and a pet cat, dog, or bird.

About half the residents of both Serbia and Montenegro live in cities, and most of those reside in either older single-family brick houses or apartment complexes. High-rise apartments are typical of suburban housing, although some well-off people can afford nice single-family homes with gardens, swimming pools, and spacious yards girded by wrought iron fences.

In the past, rural residents lived in homes that reflected the surrounding terrain. People in the Pannonian Plain tended to build homes out of mud, while those by the Adriatic coast of Montenegro favored stone. Residents of the Morava River Valley built shelters with brick, while mountain-dwellers constructed log houses. Some of these older homes can still be seen in sparsely populated areas. However, generally speaking, concrete and brick are the norm throughout the nation nowadays.

Food

Anyone looking for a filling meal will have plenty of luck in Serbia and Montenegro, although eating might be a bit tough for vegetarians. The most popular regional dishes are based on meat. In Vojvodina it is Hungarian goulash. In Montenegro it is lamb. Turkish kebabs are specialties in Kosovo. Grilled meats of all sorts are popular in Serbia. Traditional favorites are *pljeskavica*, which is a spicy hamburger steak; ražnjići, pork or veal shish kebabs with peppers and onions; and čevapčići, another type of kebab but using a spiced minced meat.

It seems that Serbs and Montenegrins will eat almost any type of meat, including pork, mutton, beef, or chicken. One special culinary delight is a "wedding feast cabbage," made from big cabbage chunks and a wide variety of meats and spices; the concoction is then boiled for at least 12 hours. Other popular meat meals include *kapama*, stewed lamb with onions and spinach served together with yogurt; *sarma*, cabbage leaves stuffed with ground meat, rice, and spices; *pršut*, or smoked ham; and *pihtije*, jellied pork or duck. Fish lovers, meanwhile, will want to sample *alaska čorba* (fishermen's stew), a requested item in Vojvodina, and filled with fish that once swam in the Danube River.

Yet there are options for diners who avoid meat. The most popular salad is Srpska salata (Serbian salad), a vegetarian dish filled with peppers, onions, and tomatoes. Bread is almost as popular as meat. Wheat bread is the most common kind, but bread is also made from millet and barley, especially in mountain villages. A treat is *pogača*, a bread made without yeast and eaten on special occasions. All visitors to Montenegro should sample a taste of *kajmak*, a local cream cheese made from salted, boiled milk.

A TASTE OF AMERICA: McDONALD'S IN SERBIA AND MONTENEGRO

When McDonald's opened its second restaurant in what was then Yugoslavia in 1989, it was at the time the largest McDonald's in the world. The eatery was located in the federal capital of Belgrade, staffed by Serbs, and had seating for 400 people on two levels. Since then bigger McDonald's restaurants have opened in Moscow, Russia, and Beijing, China, and the McDonald's chain now has a total of 16 restaurants in Serbia. McDonald's also has a mobile unit that travels to Montenegro during summer vacation periods.

McDonald's has become not just a place to grab a quick meal but also a symbol of the United States and western culture. When the huge McDonald's opened in Belgrade, Serbs enthusiastically welcomed it, greeting it as a symbol of capitalism and a chance to move forward after decades of life under Communism.

During the NATO bombings of Belgrade in 1999, angry Serb mobs showed their anger at the United States and the West by vandalizing McDonald's restaurants across Serbia, breaking windows, smashing cash registers, and wrecking kitchens. When McDonald's employees sealed off the entrance doors to prevent vandals from damaging any more property, crowds of Serbs dotted the restaurants' exteriors with anti-American graffiti. One Serbian McDonald's restaurant manager confessed, "We realized that people thought we represent[ed] America and in many ways the damage was expected."

McDonald's executives felt the best reaction was to change their image among Serbs. They declared that they will donate one dinar (about six cents) to the Serbian Red Cross for every McDonald's customer they serve. A poster on the wall of a Belgrade McDonald's depicted a traditional green Serbian hat hanging from one of McDonald's trademark golden arches juxtaposed with the Serbian flag. These efforts toward appeasing the Serbs seemed to work: One 23-year-old customer who returned to McDonald's while the Kosovo war was raging in 1999 stated, "I hate America now (but) I don't see McDonald's as an American symbol, because our people made this food."

As main courses might be hard on vegetarians, desserts can be tough on any person trying to lose weight. Most are rich and sweet, including all sorts of cakes and regional specialties such as *štrukli*, or boiled cheese balls filled with plums and nuts; *alva*, a mixture of crushed nuts and honey; and Turkish delight, jellied candies covered with powdered sugar.

Among the drinks one will find here include regional brandies, such as *šljivovica*, or peach brandy, and *vinjak*, or grape brandy. If you ask for coffee, you will most likely be served Turkish coffee, which is said to be "black and hell, strong as death, and sweet as love." In major cities, such as Belgrade, one can find any of the world's most famous brands of soft drinks, such as Coca Cola and Pepsi.

Dining habits in Serbia and Montenegro are fairly similar to those in North America, with three daily meals—breakfast, lunch, and dinner. In rural areas, farm workers favor five meals on the warm summer days, with small collations worked in between breakfast and lunch, then lunch and dinner. Busy people who would rather eat quickly have options, too: The most popular fast food in the nation is *burek*, a pastry stuffed with either cottage cheese or minced meat.

An offshoot of traditional *burek* is called *krompiruša* and is filled with potatoes. *Burek* is sold at bakeries, hamburger stands, and kiosks in the cities. Common American fast food has made its way into Serbia and Montenegro; McDonald's, Wendy's, and Burger King restaurants can all be found here.

Education

Schools have been around for a long time in Serbia and Montenegro. The earliest written records relating to education in the region date to the ninth century, when famous Christian missionaries Cyril and Methodius opened a school. For the next thousand years, education in this region had a Christian bent and took place mainly in monasteries. By the early 18th century, some Serbs who had emigrated to Austria opened secular higher schools there. By the early 19th century, with the rebirth of Serb pride, many secular institutions of learning began to open in Serbia proper. One educational center, called the Great School, opened in 1808 and would eventually evolve into the University of Belgrade. It was originally founded, according to the University of Belgrade staff, to provide "three-year studies for the needs of rebellious Serbia."

From the 1880s through the years immediately following World War I, mandatory education consisted of four years and applied only to boys. Between the two world wars, four years of education became compulsory for girls, too. After World War II, mandatory education was increased from four to eight years.

Today, eight years is still the law in both Serbia and Montenegro, although 95 percent of students go on to high school, and the majority of those students graduate. Most adults in Serbia and Montenegro's cities are well educated. But in rural areas, especially those inhabited by ethnic Albanian Muslims and parts of Kosovo, education for girls is de-emphasized since girls are generally believed to be better suited to housework or farmwork. Perhaps the major problem faced by Serb and Montenegrin educators today is "brain drain"—the departure of the brightest high school and college graduates to work better paying jobs elsewhere.

The biggest of the nation's universities is the University of Belgrade, which has an enrollment of slightly more than 65,000 undergraduate students and 2,500 graduate students. The university boasts 30 individual colleges and eight scientific institutes. It grew from the humble Great School, born in 1808, and was officially founded nearly a century later, in 1905.

The nation's smaller republic has its own state educational institution of higher learning, the University of Montenegro. Significantly smaller than its counterpart in the north, the university has an enrollment of about 9,300 students. It is also newer, founded in 1974, and contains 14 different colleges. In addition to standard colleges, such as economics, law, engineering, drama, and medicine, it also takes advantage of its seaside location by hosting what it technically refers to as a maritime faculty. Students in this department can earn degrees in marine engineering, nautical studies, and tourist studies.

Some of the nation's other universities include the University of Kragujevac and the University of Niš, both located in Serbia proper and both fairly new. The University of Kragujevac came into existence in 1976. Some of its 10 colleges were originally branches of the University of Belgrade, which gradually united with the University of Kragujevac. The university has about 8,500 students.

The University of Niš, in east-central Serbia, was founded in 1965 and today has 13 colleges. It continues to grow. In 2000 it added five new departments: geography and biology with ecology; philosophy; pedagogy; Slavic and Balkan studies; and fine arts, which became an entirely separate college in 2002.

The autonomous district of Vojvodina's biggest center of higher education is the University of Novi Sad, founded in 1960. While the campus is centered in Novi Sad, unlike most other universities, four of its 13 colleges are scattered in three other cities of Vojvodina: The colleges of civil engineering and economics are in Subotica, while the college of technical engineering is in Zrenjanin, and the teachers' training facility is in Sambor.

Kosovo has the University of Priština, which was founded in 1970 as a bilingual educational institution for the majority ethnic Albanians and minority Serbs, and it has become as famous as a hotbed of student protests as for its academics. Many of the problems began in 1990 when the Serbian government repealed then-current education legislation passed by the Kosovo parliament and dropped Albanian curricula in Kosovo's public schools and at the university. The next year the Albanian language was banned as the university's main language, and hundreds of ethnic faculty members, as well as 20,000 Albanian students, were banned from campus.

Despite ongoing negotiations between Kosovo's Ibrahim Rugova and Serbia's Slobodan Milošević, ethnic Albanian students and teachers continued to be barred from the university. On October 1, 1997, some 20,000 ethnic Albanian students protested for the right to return to the university. As NATO bombing raids began on March 24, 1999, the entire university was shut down. Finally, with a new political administration in place, the university was reopened for classes in 2001.

Dress

If you come to Serbia and Montenegro expecting to see residents in colorful folk dress, you will likely be disappointed. People here dress the same way as those in western Europe and the United States. Men wear jackets and ties and women wear dresses or other styles of business outfits

A Serbian man dons traditional dress in this photo taken between 1880 and 1924. (Courtesy Library of Congress)

to work. Young people wear casual attire, including jeans and T-shirts, just as they do elsewhere.

The best places to see Serbs and Montenegrins in traditional folk dress are religious and national festivals, where people wear old-style clothing for show and as a source of ethnic pride. One might also find tour guides in cultural or history museums and even some elderly people in remote villages wearing folk costumes.

Until the end of the 1800s, most fabric was handmade by women, who used it to craft clothing for themselves and their families. With the advent of mechanical looms in the 19th century, clothes were manufactured professionally, which only enhanced the beauty of native attire. Some Serbs and Montenegrins say the golden age of elegance in clothing was the end of the 19th century.

Costumes differed depending on the region of the country. Basically, though, men wore tanned cow leather shoes, with the tip upturned at the toes, and fastened to the legs by leather strips called *opanci*. In Vojvodina it was common for men to wear rubber shoes or boots instead. Socks, called *nazuvice*, were usually made of knitted wool and ornamented with elaborate patterns. Pants, called *čakšire*, were similar to old style knickerbockers, like those worn by Dutch settlers in colonial New York, extended to the knee where they were gathered and banded; they were held up by wide, decorative sashes, or *tkanice*.

Shirts were white and made of linen or silk and often covered by a lined, long-sleeved jacket braided with cord (*anterija*) or a waterproof cloth jacket (*gunj*) depending on the season. What men wore on their heads also depended on the season. In winter or rainy seasons, they used hooded capes of leather or some other strong material. In other places, they wore a fur cap called a *šubara*. At other times, they wore a type of soldier's cap called a *šajkača*.

Women wore *opanci* on their feet, plaited or gathered embroidered linen skirts, and *tkanice* as belts. Among the most important parts of women's folk costumes were aprons, called *pregača*, adorned with floral designs. In some areas skirts and aprons were replaced by knee-length red or blue sleeveless dresses with buttons in the front. Women wore scarves around their necks and caps fringed with cords on their heads. In some places they wore collars or strings of gold coins or caps garnished with coins or flowers.

Leisure and Sports

Serbs and Montenegrins entertain themselves as most Americans and western Europeans do. People go out to see movies and theater or concerts, and Serbia has a large number of live entertainment and movie theaters for children. But when it comes down to it, the most popular form of entertainment is television. While a lot of Serbia and Montenegro's television programs are made locally, many are imported from other nations.

Probably the second most popular form of entertainment is the home party, especially among young people. When not at home with friends, young people favor night clubs, including discos, or local dances thrown by cultural organizations. Almost all communities have festivals every year, which are well suited for families but also attract people of all ages. Of course, there are special occasions, such as weddings, birthdays, and anniversaries, all wonderful excuses for family members to get together.

Sports are also a top draw for people to either watch or participate in. Residents of Belgrade joke that every city block has either a sports arena

ONE FULL-FLEDGED AND ONE RISING STAR

Serbs and Montenegrins may be known at home for stellar soccer players, but in the United States they are most highly regarded for producing basketball players. It makes sense then that the best-known Serb or Montenegrin athlete in the United States is National Basketball Association veteran Vlade Divać. The center, born in Prijepolje, Serbia, in 1968, has played for three NBA teams and is recognized as one of the most versatile centers in the game. Standing 7'1" and weighing 260 pounds. Divać is respected as a skilled shooter, rebounder, shot blocker, and passer.

Divać played professional basketball for five years in Yugoslavia before being drafted by the Los Angeles Lakers in 1989. Legendary Lakers star Kareem Abdul-Jabbar had just retired, and the Lakers needed a new center. After sharing the duties with Mychal Thompson for one year, Divać became the Lakers' full-time center. He constantly made the league's statistical lists of top players. In the 1993–94 season he ranked 12th in the NBA with 40 double-doubles. In one game that season, he grabbed 24 rebounds, the most for a Laker since Abdul-Jabbar pulled down 25 in 1979.

When the Lakers purchased free-agent center Shaquille O'Neal in 1996, Divać was traded to the Charlotte Hornets for the draft rights to young Kobe Bryant. Divać took time off that year to play basketball for Yugoslavia in the 1996 Summer Olympics in Atlanta, Georgia, leading his homeland to the silver medal. Before the 1998 season he was traded to the Sacramento Kings, and he has helped them become a perpetual playoff contender.

Off the court, the dark-bearded center runs the Divać Fund, which he founded, whose goal is to raise money to help children hurt by the Yugoslav civil war. He and his wife have adopted a daughter who was born in Belgrade.

Waiting in the wings to perhaps become the next Vlade Divać is Darko Miličić, another Serb native. Born in Novi Sad in 1985, Miličić stands 7 feet tall and weighs 245 pounds. He started playing basketball at age 10 just to spend more time with friends but at age 14 realized how talented he was and began to take the pastime more seriously. Since Serbia and Montenegro has no structured high school basketball system, and since Miličić was too young to play on Serbia and Montenegro's national team, Miličić's parents signed their son—then age 15—to a professional contract with a team called KK Hemofarm in a professional Serbian league.

The current NBA player Miličić has been compared to most is Minnesota Timberwolves' forward Kevin Garnett. They are about the same size, have long arms, and are adept ball handlers and passers. Miličić is known for being humble but not scared to be aggressive when necessary, a skill he learned from playing mostly against adults. Pat Burke, center for the Orlando Magic, played against Miličić in Europe in 2002. Burke said a year later, "My first thought was, 'I'm 28 and here I am playing against a high school kid.' But I was impressed right away. He was a lot better at 16 than a lot of players at the end of their pro careers. Nothing but positives will happen for him."

In the NBA draft of June 2003, Miličić was the second player chosen overall, selected by the Detroit Pistons.

Serbia's Vlade Divać, left, a star for many years in the National Basketball Association (NBA) in the United States, raises his arm in victory after Team Yugoslavia's 84–77 win over Argentina in the Gold Medal game of the 2002 World Basketball championships held in Indianapolis. To the right is Divać's teammate Marko Jarić. (AP Photo/ Michael Conroy)

or stadium. Belgrade's biggest stadium seats 60,000 fans; the biggest arena in the city has a capacity of 7,000.

The most popular sport is soccer, referred to as "football" in Europe, with basketball not far behind. Soccer dates back longer, introduced into Serbia by local students returning from Switzerland in the late 1800s. The first soccer club in the nation was founded in Belgrade in 1903. Belgrade's first official basketball game took place in 1923, just 32 years after the game was invented in Springfield, Massachusetts. Yugoslavia's soccer and basketball teams have earned Olympic medals on numerous occasions. Its soccer team won the gold in 1960; silver in 1948, 1952, and 1956; and a bronze in 1984. The Olympic basketball team won the gold in 1980; silvers in 1968, 1976, 1988, and 1996; and a bronze in 1984. In a major upset, the Yugoslav national team beat Team USA in the quarterfinals of the 2002 World Championships held in Indianapolis, Indiana.

Serbia has also produced Olympic champions in other sports, such as volleyball, handball, water polo, and judo, while rising tennis star Jelena Dokić, born in Belgrade in 1983, has beaten some of the biggest names in the sport, including Venus Williams and Martina Hingis. Montenegrins are best known for their standout soccer players. Montenegrin forwards Dejan Savičević and Predrag Mijatović are among the best-known soccer stars in Europe.

NOTES

p. 119 "'For some people . . .'" "goga4444's Serbia and Montenegro Page," Virtual-Tourist. Available on-line. URL: http://www.virtualtourist.com/m/3b62e/4bc/. Downloaded May 25, 2003.

p. 120 "'I just want people . . .'" "goga 4444's Serbia and Montenegro Page."

p. 120 "'When I went to Canada . . .'" "South-Slavia's Serbia and Montenegro Page," VirtualTourist. Available on-line. URL:http://www.virtualtourist.com/m/22673/4bc/. Downloaded May 25, 2003.

p. 122 "When McDonald's opened . . ." "Welcome to McDonald's in Yugoslavia," McDonald's. Available on-line. URL: http://www.mcdonalds.com/countries/yugoslavia/index.html. Downloaded June 2, 2003.

p. 122 "One Serbian McDonald's restaurant manager . . ." J. G. Freund, "Giving NATO the Middle Finger," salon.com. (April 26, 1999) Available on-line. URL: http://www.salon.com/news/feature/1999/04/26/belgrade/indes1.html. Downloaded June 2, 2003.

p. 122 "One 23-year-old customer . . ." Freund, "Giving NATO the Middle Finger."

p. 123 "If you ask for coffee . . ." *Lonely Planet: Eastern Europe* Oakland, Calif.: Lonely Planet Publications, 1999, p. 801.

pp. 123–124 "It was originally founded . . ." "Foundation and development," University of Belgrade. Available on-line. URL: http://www.bg.ac.yu/main. Downloaded June 4, 2003.

p. 124 "Today, eight years is still the law . . ." "Who are Serbs?" St. Vuk Stefanovich Karadzich. Available on-line. URL: http://www.serbialinks.freehosting.net/serbs.htm. Downloaded May 25, 2003.

p. 129 "Burke said a year later . . ." David Dupree, "Serbian teen lost in King James' shadow," *USA Today*, April 1, 2003, p. 3c.

9

CITIES

Modern industry and ancient ruins are the hallmarks of the cities of Serbia and Montenegro. Even though some communities suffered significant damage due to the 1999 bombing attacks, they are currently in the rebuilding process. It is not easy, and many residents of Belgrade and Novi Sad still hold onto bitter feelings toward the NATO nations. However, these cities have been around for centuries, and their citizens are hardly ready to give up.

Belgrade

Once the capital of the entire Kingdom of Serbs, Croats, and Slovenes, then the capital of the six-republic nation of Yugoslavia, Belgrade is a world-class city with more than 1.5 million people. It has long been the spiritual heart of the Serbian people. Of the total population, about 92 percent, or all but about 130,000 residents, are of Serb ancestry.

Belgrade suffered mightily from NATO bombings in 1999, but its mayor, Radmila Hrustanović, said in 2001 that her top priority was to return Belgrade to its status as a world capital. She announced, "My first task is putting in order all public utility systems. Maybe just because I am a woman, the most important goal for me is a clean Belgrade! And clean Belgrade means healthier Belgrade." She added, "I shall do everything for Belgrade to become at last beautiful, clean, peaceful, and safe, a modern city of the world! I will take care of Belgrade like I take care of my family and my children."

The capital city sits in the north-central part of Serbia proper, at the point where the Sava River empties into the Danube River and just across the border from Vojvodina. Because it is surrounded by water on three sides, it has since ancient times been considered the "guardian of river passages," "the gate" of the Balkans, and "the door" to central Europe.

It is also a heavily industrial city. Industry accounts for the biggest share, 29 percent, of the city's economy. Energy power plants dot the landscape, and factories in Belgrade manufacture everything from machine tools to microelectronics to shoes to medicine.

As a major European capital, the city is home to 196 elementary schools, 82 secondary schools, 59 health institutions, including hospitals and clinics, and some of the finest museums in the Balkans, of which the biggest are devoted to different aspects of Serbian heritage. These include the Ethnographical Museum, which maintains a superb collection of folk costumes and folk art, and the National Museum, stocked with archaeological displays and priceless works of European art.

The Military Museum is located on the grounds of the medieval-style Kalemegdan Citadel. (Although a fortress of some sort has occupied the space since the days of the Celts, most of the current structure was built in the 17th century.) This museum has 53 rooms, which are utilized to tell virtually the entire story of Yugoslav history. Tourists might also want to see the grave of Marshal Tito, buried on the grounds of his former home on Bulevar Mira.

When Belgrade's residents are not at work, they might be found reading a book, riding a bicycle, or taking a swim in Ada Ciganlija, the city's grandest park, located on an island in the Sava River; there is even a spot in the park set aside for skinny-dipping in the Sava. Locals can also be found mixing among the tourists and shopping along the Kneza Mihaila, a pedestrian mall in the heart of downtown.

A night out on the town could mean taking in the opera at the National Theater, a music concert at the Serbian Academy of Arts and Sciences, or dancing to the latest music from Europe and America's recording studios at a disco, such as Club Promocija. There is a Hard Rock Café in the city, too. The citizens of Belgrade are not formal about dressing for an evening out. Jeans are acceptable nearly everywhere, even at the opera.

Novi Sad

A municipality of about 200,000, Novi Sad is the political and commercial capital of Vojvodina. However, sports fans around the world know Novi Sad best as the birthplace of tennis great Monica Seles.

Located in southern Vojvodina, Novi Sad was founded in 1670, making it by European standards practically a brand-new community. The city has long taken advantage of its location on the banks of the Danube River by being home to a busy port. Like Belgrade, it is also an industrial center, with factories producing textiles, processed foods, and electrical equipment. Novi Sad is also home to a major oil refinery.

This midsized city displays a distinct Hungarian influence, which makes sense considering that it was part of the Austro-Hungarian Empire until 1918. The first thing most visitors notice about downtown Novi Sad is that its center, the Trg Slobode (Square of Liberty), takes the form of a star, with five main streets emanating from it, all in different directions.

While Novi Sad is not home to buildings with medieval roots like many other European communities, it does have its share of historic buildings, which draw tourists. One is the majestic synagogue, built in 1909 and housing an auditorium with acoustics so fine that it is still used for concerts. Another is the Banovina, where Vojvodina's executive council meets. The Banovina dates to 1939 and is basically made from marble; its exterior marble is from the Croatian island of Brač, while its staircases and central hall are covered with *carara* marble from Italy. Some of the side roads, such as Laze Telećkog Street and Svetozara Miletica Street, are home to clusters of architecturally intriguing buildings, including banks and private residences, dating to the 1800s.

But probably the most visited Novi Sad landmark is the city's oldest. The Petrovaradin Citadel was constructed in two phases over the course of nearly nine decades, from 1692 to 1780. Nicknamed the "Gibraltar of the Danube," the immense fortress complex consists today of a plush hotel, a restaurant, two small museums, and a large church connected by stairs to the fortified section at its summit. It has also become the city's art center, with studios and cafés incorporated into the complex. It is common to see locals and visitors alike strolling atop the citadel walls, enjoying the inspiring view of the Danube River, the compact downtown, and the surrounding countryside in the distance.

Novi Sad was the site of three bridges over the Danube, which were destroyed in April 1999 during the NATO bombing attacks, and the city's residents are still angered about their destruction. However, within a year, the Varadin Bridge (formerly known as Marshal Tito's Bridge) was rebuilt. The city's officials are debating how to approach rebuilding the other two bridges.

Niš

Niš, located in south-southeastern Serbia proper, is one of the most ancient cities in the Balkans and, with 300,000 inhabitants, is the second largest municipality in Serbia and Montenegro. According to local legend, it was founded by a Slavic prince named Niša, and it was first built with local Humska Cuka stone, but archaeological digs have shown that this spot was actually inhabited in prehistoric times. For a long time it was an important military crossroads, proven by existing records dating from the second century.

Like Belgrade and Novi Sad, Niš has its own industrial section. It is well known in the Balkans for its electronics, textile, and tobacco plants. Niš's 30 health-care facilities serve all the residents of southeastern Serbia and include a medical facility affiliated with the University of Niš. It is also a midsized cultural center with a national theater, a puppet theater in which classic south Slavic fairy tales are interpreted, and an award-winning children's theater. It is also a venue for annual film and music festivals.

Priština

Priština is the capital of and largest city in the autonomous district of Kosovo. With the flow of refugees out of and then back into Priština following the 1999 Kosovo War, it is hard to know exactly how many people live in Priština today. Estimates of the current population generally center around 105,000.

Priština's roots go back to Roman times. Remains of an Illyrian community called Ulpina have been discovered southeast of Priština, and artifacts, such as coins, weapons, jewelry, and ceramics, from the area are on view at Priština's Museum of Kosovo. But while Priština has been trying to return to some semblance of normalcy, the fact that the museum is now being used as headquarters for the European Agency for Reconstruction shows that there is still a long way to go.

Because the Battle of Kosovo Polje of 1389 was fought near the city, Priština has a special place in the hearts and minds of Serbs. But its overall style is definitely Turkish-Islamic. Walk down Priština's narrow, winding, and unpaved roads and one will discover Turkish baths, 13 mosques, and shops selling filigree jewelry or other regionally made handcrafts. One of the region's most popular natural attractions is the Marble Cave, consisting of marble cliffs formed by the metamorphosis of limestone, a colorful and rare phenomenon. It is located about 20 miles south of Priština, in the village of Gadimlje.

The residents of Priština are trying to host tourists again, but many westerners still associate Kosovo with war and bombings. Indeed, there are still some intensely poor areas in the city. But Priština residents maintain hope for the future.

Podgorica

Since the Illyrian age, there have been settlements of some type on the site of Podgorica, the political, cultural, and economic capital of the Republic of Montenegro. Located in south-central Montenegro, Podgorica, population 117,000, was given its current name in 1326 after the nearby hill called Gorica. In 1946 it was renamed Titograd, after then-president Tito. The name *Podgorica* was reinstated on April 2, 1992.

Slow to industrialize, Podgorica did not get its first significant commercial business until 1902, when a tobacco processing factory opened. Still, it remained a fairly sleepy town until July 13, 1946, when as Titograd it became the republic's capital. In the time that followed, industry and educational and health institutions moved in. During the same period, the building of modern roads and the commencement of air travel linked the city to both the rest of Montenegro and to foreign countries and turned Podgorica into an important, if somewhat small, metropolis.

The most recognizable symbol of the city is the tall, stone clock tower, and its most important cultural institution is the Palace of the Petrović, a

Children in Negrovce, Kosovo, attend math class in an unfinished building in September 1999. The main school building was destroyed by Serbs earlier in the year during the Serb-Kosovan conflict. (AP Photo/Adam Butler)

former 19th-century winter mansion and today a showcase for contemporary art. Painters from Montenegro as well as artists from foreign nations, such as India, Cuba, Venezuela, Uganda, and Cyprus, have had a chance to showcase their art on the palace walls. Podgorica is also an open trade center, and its stores commonly offer for sale first-class imported clothes, especially those made by some of the famous designers from Italy.

Cetinje

While Podgorica is the de facto capital of Montenegro, Cetinje might be considered the republic's spiritual capital. This small city, population around 20,000, actually once was its official capital. Montenegrins have written songs and poems about the storied city for centuries. Outside of the beach resorts, such as Budva and Sveti Stefan, it might be the community most frequently visited by tourists.

Cetinje, located a bit inland from the Adriatic Sea, has been welcoming visitors since 1808, when its first tourist facility, an inn owned by a senator named Milo Martinović, was constructed. Tourism has grown and wavered many times since then, depending on political and economic conditions. Today, nearly every traveler takes time to step inside the famous Cetinje Monastery, with its rare *Oktoih*, the *Book of the Eight Voices*, printed near this spot in 1494, when the monastery was just 10 years old.

Most also want to see the older, stately palace of Montenegro's last king, Nikola I Petrović, built in 1871 and today serving as the State Museum. Unfortunately, much of the palace was looted during World War II, but a representation of period artifacts give visitors a sense of Nikola's time. Just 12 miles away from Cetinje is Mt. Lovćen, called Montenegro (Black Mountain) in Italian, which was the inspiration for the republic's name.

NOTES

p. 133 "Of the total population . . ." "Facts about Belgrade: Population," City of Belgrade. Available on-line. URL: http://www.beograd.org.yu/english/grad/cinjenic/stanovn.htm. Downloaded June 9, 2003.

pp. 133–134 "She announced, 'My first . . .'" "Belgrade—My City," City of Belgrade. Available on-line. URL: http://www.beograd.org.yu/english/zivot/mojgrad/index.htm. Downloaded June 9, 2003.

p. 134 "Industry accounts for the biggest share . . ." "Economy and Business: Economic Potentials," City of Belgrade. Available on-line. URL: http://www.beograd.org.yu/english/zivot/ekonom/potenc/indust.htm. Downloaded June 9, 2003.

PRESENT PROBLEMS AND FUTURE SOLUTIONS

Serbia and Montenegro has faced more changes in the last 15 years than many nations go through in a century. First, these two republics were part of a bigger country that disintegrated into smaller sections. As the last remaining unit of Yugoslavia, it aggressively participated in two civil wars. Then the nation itself almost broke into two parts.

For almost an entire decade, it was a pariah nation, isolated politically and economically from much of the rest of the world. Its capital and other cities were targets of bombing missions, and much of its infrastructure was destroyed. It has since tried to restructure as a democracy and make allies in the rest of the world; in the meantime, it has also changed its name, constitution, and government structure.

What Is Going Right

First of all, there is peace. There is certainly residual anger among the nation's citizens, but no active fighting is taking place. The NATO nations have not bombed Belgrade since 1999, and the Serbian military is no longer hunting down rebellious Kosovans. Ethnic cleansing is an activity of the past. New governments in place in Serbia and Montenegro are making determined efforts to keep the peace.

On July 15, 2002, the leaders of the former warring nations met for the first time since the end of the civil war. They vowed to cooperate with each other and work hard to instill peace in the once-troubled area. Croatia's president Stipe Mesić announced at the Sarajevo meeting, "Behind us is a brutal war which has left heavy consequences. Europe is integrating and that's our destiny, too. We want to cooperate with Bosnia-Herzegovina and with Yugoslavia."

However, not all ill will has been erased. At that historic meeting, Beriz Belkić, the Muslim chairman of Bosnia's presidency, said publicly that he wanted an apology from Serbia for the atrocities committed against Bosnians during the war. In response, Yugoslav president Vojislav Koštunica insisted that since there was no need for him to apologize, he was not about to do so.

The Lingering Question of War Criminals

While the United Nation's International Criminal Tribunal for the Former Yugoslavia (ICTY), has jurisdiction for persons accused of war crimes, crimes against humanity, and genocide that took place during the Yugoslav civil war, there is one thing it cannot do: hunt down and arrest suspects. The Bosnians, Croatians, and NATO nations have been in an ongoing battle with Belgrade to locate and turn over suspects, and their perceived lack of cooperation in this regard has caused consternation among other nations. Some journalists based in the Balkans say that some wanted war criminals still at large, such as Ratko Mladić, allegedly involved in the massacre of Muslim civilians at Srebrenica in 1995, "continue to enjoy wide public support in Serbia."

However, the new government of Serbia and Montenegro has declared that it will from now on fully cooperate with the ICTY as necessary. On June 6, 2003, in Washington, D.C., Serbia and Montenegro's ambassador Ivan Vujačić stated in a briefing on Democracy, Human Rights and Justice in Serbia that his country is actively obtaining documents and conducting hearings in order to locate witnesses and indicted persons. Vujačić stated. "The respect for human rights is the essence of our civilization. We have done a great deal, much remains to be done. We want to live in a country in which people know and stand up for their rights, and perhaps more importantly the rights of others. Given the history, we have a long way to go, but certainly, we are on the right road and there is no turning back."

In addition to the election of a new government, the assassination of Serbia's reformist prime minister Zoran Djindjić appeared to be a major turning point in the Serbs' change in attitude. Thirty-six suspected representatives of organized crime and members of an elite police unit were charged with the murder. When the trial began on December 22, 2003, 14 suspects were still at large, including the alleged mastermind of the assassination, Milorad Luković, who commanded the Red Berets during the Balkan wars. NATO secretary general George Robertson said that Djindjić's murder was a "desperate action by violent extremists who want to return to Milošević authoritarianism."

Poverty

As stated in the economy chapter, it has been estimated that 30 percent of the population of Serbia and Montenegro live in poverty. Experts also say that as many as half of the people of Kosovo live in poverty.

There are several reasons for these high rates. First, there have always been relatively high numbers of poor Serbs and Montenegrins as compared to the other Yugoslav republics, and Kosovo has always been near the bottom. Secondly, Kosovo is going through a transition period from emergency relief to longer-term development, so a solid and detailed development plan will have to be designed and put into effect.

Thirdly, time, money, and resources are still being invested to complete the rebuilding of the infrastructure of Belgrade and other municipalities damaged by NATO bombs in 1999. One additional reason for the lofty poverty rate is that Serbia and Montenegro were on the global outside for 10 years, and it will take time to be fully reintegrated into the regional and international economies.

One step toward the reduction of the massive poverty rate is an influx of foreign capital as businesses based in other nations open offices or factories in Serbia and Montenegro, creating jobs for the unemployed. In addition to Malcolm Bricklin's renewed interest in distributing Yugos, the European division of an American company, Ball Packaging Europe, announced in January 2003 that it will open a beverage tin can factory in the town of Zemun. This Serbia-based plant is expected to produce about 600 million tin cans a year, with 80 percent being exported to other Eastern European nations. Ball Packaging Europe ultimately hopes to employ about 300 people in the factory.

The private sector aside, the World Bank of the United Nations has announced a plan to reduce by half the poverty level in Serbia and Montenegro by 2015. As part of the United Nations's Millennium Development Goals, which are targets the body has set to reduce poverty throughout the world by 2015, an aggressive new program to attack poverty in the two republics was prepared in 2001. Already, UN agencies, such as the United Nations Development Program (UNDP) and the United Nations High Commissioner for Refugees (UNHCR), have started to reallocate their funds from construction projects, such as roads and bridges, toward programs that will directly target poverty.

Refugees

One of the most heart-wrenching problems throughout Serbia, as well as Bosnia and Herzegovina and Croatia, is that of refugees and internally displaced persons. The Kosovo situation was immensely complex, both logistically and politically. For example, since Kosovo is politically a part of Serbia, Kosovans who escaped to Serbia during the 1999 war are technically not refugees; they considered to be internally displaced persons.

It has been reported that the 1999 Kosovo War resulted in both the fastest exodus and quickest return of refugees in modern history. The United Nations has stated that an estimated 880,000 Kosovars either fled or were deported to nearby nations, then returned just a few months later, as soon as the fighting had ended. And just after the war was over, approximately 230,000 Serbs and Roma fled Kosovo for Serbia and Montenegro or Macedonia. By 2003 the overwhelming majority of those were living either outside of Kosovo or in makeshift refugee camps in Kosovo set up specifically to house returning refugees.

Several hundred Roma are currently living in a few dozen dilapidated homes constructed of mud bricks, with plastic sheets or cardboard as

Hordes of ethnic Albanian refugees arrive by tractor in the village of Jablanica, Montenegro, on April 5, 1999. These were just some of the estimated 350,000 ethnic Albanians who poured into neighboring states from Kosovo during the 1999 war. (AP Photo/Pier Paolo Cito)

roofs, in a refugee settlement outside of the Serbian town of Požarevac. They are scared to return to their homes because they do not feel safe there; because of their legal status as internally displaced persons, however, they cannot find employment in Požarevac. Many of them eke out a living by scrounging bottles and cardboard from garbage cans, then reselling them. Many dwellers in the camp are not even sure if the homes they left are still standing.

An area Romani organization, called Rom, was at one time a source for food and clothing for the refugees, but Rom officials say they no longer have the financial or material resources to continue helping in this manner. One Romani camp resident, Ali Berisha, lives with 12 other people in a shack and sleeps on mattresses on the ground. Berisha wondered,

"What am I living for? I search through the trash for some bread for my children. In the trash I try to find some meat to bring home. We came from Kosovo, it doesn't mean that we came from America; we are not foreigners. It seems to me that we are Yugoslavs."

Thankfully, relief is on it way from a number of sources. The Norwegian Refugee Council has fought for the rights of refugees from the former Yugoslav republics mainly by using the court system. The council has provided free legal aid for refugees in Serbia since 1997 and from Kosovo since 1999. Some of its accomplishments have included operating legal aid projects, resulting in informing refugees and internally displaced persons of their legal rights; contributing building materials for the homes of refugees who have already begun the integration process; expanding the capacity of group homes for elderly refugees; and helping local groups, especially those related to legal aid, to improve civilian society in Kosovo.

In the same vein, the Organization for Security and Cooperation in Europe (OSCE) Mission to Serbia and Montenegro and the Council of Europe jointly sponsored in March 2003 a Belgrade seminar for lawyers whose jobs are to help refugees and internally displaced persons return to their homes. With rapidly changing political situations and complex laws in the former Yugoslav republics, the purpose of the seminar was to help outline and clarify means within the European Convention on Human Rights to help refugees go home.

Financial aid is arriving, too. In March 2003 the European Commission granted 6.66 million euros (about $7.83 million) in humanitarian aid to refugees and displaced persons in Serbia and Montenegro. The money was earmarked toward the distribution of basic food packages for 50,000 displaced persons and about 118,000 refugees in Serbia.

And in May 2003, the United States committed $14.4 million specifically for the return of displaced persons and refugees to Kosovo. The money was sent to nongovernment organizations, such as the American Rescue Committee, International Catholic Migration Commission, United Methodist Committee on Relief, and Mercy Corps. The head of the United States Mission in Priština, Reno Harnish, said at the time, "It is now up to community and political leaders in Kosovo, Serbia-Montenegro, and Macedonia to work together constructively to resolve property claims, to help people move back to their homes if they wish to do so, or to integrate into those communities where they now reside, if that is their choice."

NOTES

p. 142 "Croatia's president Stipe Mesić announced . . ." "Balkan heads vow to rebuild peace," CNN. (July 15, 2002) Available on-line. URL: www.cnn.com/2002/WORLD/europe/07/15/balkans.summit/index.html. Downloaded March 8, 2003.

p. 142 "Some journalists based in the Balkans . . ." R. Jeffrey Smith, "Assassination in Belgrade Costs U.S. a Powerful Ally," Washington Post. (March 13, 2003) Available on-line. URL: http://www.washingtonpost.com/ac2/wp-dyn/A17750-2003Mar12?language=printer. Downloaded May 10, 2003.

pp. 142–143 "On June 6, 2003 . . ." "Ambassador Vujacić reiterates the commitment of Serbia and Montenegro to cooperate with the ICTY," Embassy of Serbia and Montenegro. (June 6, 2003) Available on-line. URL: http://news.serbianunity.net/bydate/2003/June_06/11.html. Downloaded June 11, 2003.

p. 143 "NATO secretary general George Robertson . . ." Smith.

p. 143 "Experts also say that . . ." "Qualitative Poverty Survey Project," United Nations Development Programme. Available on-line. URL: http://www.kosovo.undp.org/Projects/QQPS/qqps.htm. Downloaded June 9, 2003.

p. 144 "The United Nations has stated that . . ." United Nations High Commissioner for Refugees, "The *Balkans:* What Next," *Refugees* 3, no. 124:8. Available on-line. URL: http://www.unchr.org/. Downloaded June 11, 2003.

p. 144 "And just after the war was over. . . ." *Refugees*, p. 10.

pp. 145–146 "Berisha wondered . . ." Vesna Misic, translated by Natasha Petrovic, "Serbia's Roma refugees: Living out of sight," ReliefWeb. (May 28, 2003) Available on-line. URL: http://www.reliefweb.int/w/rwb.nsf/. Downloaded June 11, 2003.

p. 146 "In March 2003 the European Commission granted . . ." "Commission adopts EUR 6.66 million humanitarian aid package for Serbia," European Commission—Humanitarian Aid Office (ECHO) release, ReliefWeb. (March 18, 2003) Available on-line. URL: http://www.reliefweb.int/w/Rwb.nsf. Downloaded June 11, 2003.

p. 146 "The money was earmarked toward . . ." "Commission adopts . . ."

p. 146 "The head of the United States Mission in Priština . . ." "U.S. to supply 14 million dollars for Kosovo refugees return," Deutsche Presse Agentur, ReliefWeb. (May 7, 2003) Available on-line. URL: http://www.reliefweb.int/w/Rwb.nsf. Downloaded June 11, 2003.

CHRONOLOGY

3500 B.C.

Ancient civilization resides in what is now Serbia and Montenegro

400 B.C.

Greeks invade Illyria

200 B.C.

Romans stretch empire into Illyria

A.D. 600s

Slavic tribes enter region

626

Byzantine emperor Heraclius joins forces with Serbs, who settle inland in Balkan Peninsula

1169 or 1170

Stefan Nemanja becomes leader of Serbs

1217

Stefan Prvovenčani declared Serb king by Pope Honorius III

1330

Stefan Uroš III leads Serbs to victory over Bulgars

1389

Ottoman Empire defeats Serbs in Battle of Kosovo Polje

1422

Stefan Crnojević becomes leader of Montenegro

1516

Vladikas begin rule of Montenegro, changing government from civil leadership to theocracy

1718

Treaty of Passarowitz brings parts of Serbia under control of the Austro-Hungarian Empire

1798

Peter I establishes Montenegrin code of laws

1805

Serb rebellion under Karageorge

1815

Second Serb rebellion under peasant leader Miloš Obrenović

1878

Treaty of Berlin alters map of eastern Europe, including Serbia and Montenegro

1903

Alexander Obrenović assassinated, ending Obrenović dynasty

1912–13

Balkan Wars

1914

Archduke Francis Ferdinand of Austria-Hungary assassinated in Sarajevo triggering World War I

1917

Corfu Declaration announced, with plans to form a pan–South Slav kingdom

1918

World War I ends; Serbian crown prince Alexander forms new nation: Kingdom of Serbs, Croats, and Slovenes

1928

Stjepan Radić and two other Croat diplomats assassinated in parliament in Belgrade

1929

Alexander names himself absolute ruler of the kingdom, renamed Yugoslavia (Kingdom of the South Slavs)

1934

Alexander assassinated by member of fascist Ustaša

1935

Milan Stojadinović named prime minister by Prince Pavle

1939

Dragiša Cvetković named prime minister by Prince Pavle

1941

Nazi Germany attacks Yugoslavia two years into World War II; Yugoslavia surrenders

1941–45

Serbs, Jews, Roma, and others murdered in death camps

1943

Antifascist Council for the National Liberation of Yugoslavia, also known as the Partisans, meet in Jajce to make postwar plans

1945

Germany and Ustaša surrender; World War II ends; Marshal Tito takes over nation's leadership, employs liberalized form of Communist government referred to as Titoism; Vojvodina and Kosovo established as autonomous districts in Serbia

1961

Belgrade hosts world's first conference of nonaligned nations, at which Tito publicly denounces neocolonialism

1968

Antigovernment demonstrations take place in Serbia

1980

Tito dies; system of rotating presidents takes effect

1981–82

Ethnic Albanians in Kosovo actively protest against federal government

1983

Krajgher Commission Report released, calls for a form of free market economy in Yugoslavia

1986

Memorandum calling for Serb unity published in Belgrade newspaper

1987

Agrokomerc scandal exposes widespread corruption in Yugoslavian business; Slobodan Milošević gives powerful speech praising Serb unity; public protests in Belgrade and civil unrest in Kosovo and Vojvodina; Milošević named top Communist Party official

1989

Montenegrin leaders forced to resign, replaced by Milošević sympathizers; more than 1,900 labor strikes take place across Yugoslavia; Milošević elected leader of Serb Republic

1990

Croatian nationalist Franjo Tudjman elected president of Croatia; Serbs in Serb-dominated area of Krajina in Croatia declare autonomy

1991

March: Two killed in anti-Milošević demonstrations
June: Croatia and Slovenia secede from nation
summer and fall: Yugoslav People's Army and Serb troops gain control of Serb-dominated areas of Croatia
October: Bosnia and Herzegovina declares independence; Yugoslav president Stipe Mesić steps down, declares end of Yugoslavia

1992

March: Montenegro votes to stay in rump Yugoslavia with Serbia; Bosnia, and Herzegovina votes to declare independence; ethnic Serbs in Bosnia and Herzegovina declare own republic
spring: Ibrahim Rugova elected president of Kosovo in illegal election
summer: Reports of ethnic cleansing by Serbs first surface
December 20: Milošević wins reelection as president of Serb republic in controversial election

1993

January 10: Montenegro's president Momir Bulatović reelected

1994

February 5: 68 civilians killed by Serb mortar shell in attack on Sarajevo marketplace

1995

July: Massacre at Srebrenica
November 1: Peace talks begin at Wright-Patterson Air Force Base in Dayton, Ohio
November 21: Peace treaty agreed upon in Dayton ends war
December 14: Peace treaty signed in Paris, France

1996

Kosovo Liberation Army (KLA) forms

1997

July: Milošević elected president of Yugoslavia

October 19: Anti-Milošević candidate Milo Djukanović elected president of Montenegro

1998

February 28: Serb officials begin military campaign to destroy KLA

October 25: North Atlantic Treaty Organization (NATO) nations negotiate cease-fire in Kosovo, Organization for Security and Cooperation in Europe (OSCE) sends in peace monitors

December: Cease-fire falls apart, fighting returns to Kosovo

1999

January 15: 45 ethnic Albanians killed in Račak, Kosovo

February: Peace talks in Rambouillet, France, fail; Serb-led attacks on ethnic Albanians increase

March 24: NATO forces launch strikes against Serb military targets; Montenegro sides with NATO against Milošević

May 27: International War Crimes Tribunal (ICTY) issues warrant for arrest of Milošević

June 3: Milošević accepts NATO peace plan

June 10: NATO forces stop bombing campaign

2000

October 7: Vojislav Koštunica elected president of Yugoslavia, defeating Milošević

2001

January: Zoran Djindjić elected first noncommunist Serb prime minister in modern times

April: Filip Vojanović elected president of Montenegro

June: Milošević turned over to ICTY

November: Ibrahim Rugova elected president of Kosovo

2002

March 14: Serbia and Montenegro agree to restructure nation and officially call it Serbia and Montenegro

July 15: Presidents of Bosnia and Herzegovina, Croatia, and Yugoslavia meet for first time since signing of Dayton peace agreement

November 29: New constitutional charter adopted

2003

February 4: New name and new nation of Serbia and Montenegro become official as new constitution is approved

March 12: Serbian prime minister Zoran Djindjić is assassinated in Belgrade; Svetozvar Marović is elected president of Serbia and Montenegro

December 28: Serbian Radical Party, an ultranationalist party, gains the most votes in parliamentary elections in Serbia

FURTHER READING

Bran, Zoe. *After Yugoslavia*. Oakland, Calif.: Lonely Planet Publications, 2001.

Corrick, James A. *The Byzantine Empire*. San Diego: Lucent Books, 1997.

Curtin, Leah. *Sunflowers in the Sand: Stories from Children of War*. Lanham, Md.: Madison Books, 1999.

Doder, Dusko, and Bronson, Louise. *Milošević: Portrait of a Tyrant*. New York: The Free Press, 1999.

Filipović, Zlata. *Zlata's Diary: A Child's Life in Sarajevo*. New York: Viking Press, 1994.

Grant, James P. *I Dream of Peace: Images of War by Children of Former Yugoslavia*. New York: HarperCollins, 1994.

Hicyilmaz, Gaye. *Smiling for Strangers*. New York: Farrar Straus Giroux, 2000.

Lindsay, Franklin. *Beacons in the Night: With the OSS and Tito's Partisans in Wartime Yugoslavia*. Stanford, Calif.: Stanford University Press, 1993.

Mead, Alice. *Adem's Cross*. New York: Farrar Straus Giroux, 1996.

————. *Girl of Kosovo*. New York: Farrar Straus Giroux, 2001.

Mertis, Julie, et al. *The Suitcase: Refugee Voices from Bosnia and Croatia*. Berkeley: University of California Press, 1997.

Ousseimi, Maria. *Caught in the Crossfire: Growing Up in a War Zone*. New York: Walker & Co., 1995.

Ross, Stewart. *Only a Matter of Time*. Hauppauge, N.Y.: Barron's, 2002.

Schiffman, Ruth. *Tito*. New York: Chelsea House, 1987.

Silber, Laura. *Yugoslavia: Death of a Nation*. New York: Penguin Books, 1997.

Simoen, Jan. *What about Anna?* New York: Walker & Company, 2002.

Strom, Yale. *Uncertain Roads: Searching for the Gypsies*. New York: Four Winds Press, 1993.

Tekavic, Valerie, et al. *Teenage Refugees from Bosnia-Herzegovina Speak Out*. New York: Rosen Publishing Group, 1997

West, Rebecca. *Black Lamb & Grey Falcon: A Journey through Yugoslavia*. New York: Viking Press, 1943.

Woog, Adam. *The United Nations*. San Diego: Lucent Books, 1994.

INDEX